D1288960

4779

Huron School Library
Huron, Ohio

MEN WHO CHANGED THE MAP

Huron School Library
Huron, Ohio

THE BRITISH

NORTH SEA OR GERMAN OCEAN

GERMAN

IRELAND

Dublin

Cork

GREAT BRITAIN

THE ENGLISH CHAN.

ST. GEORGES CHAN.

BRISTOL CHAN.

Str. of Dover

UNITED PROVINCES

WESTPHALIA

SAX.

HANOVER

THE

ATLANTIC

OCEAN

BAY OF BISCAY

Brest

FRANCE

Paris

Versailles

Orleans

Tours

Bourdeaux

Dijon

Lyons

SWITZERLAND

Suisse

SAVOY

GRISONS

PIEDMONT

MILAN

Turin

Gulf of Genoa

Leghorn

PARMA

MODENA

CORSICA

SPAIN

Madrid

Valladolid

Salamanca

Leon

Bilboa

Burgos

Pampelona

Saragosa

Barcelona

Tarragona

Ebro R.

Gulf of Lyons

Toulon

G. de la Yasse

Minorca I.

Majorca I.

Yvica I.

Valencia

Alicant

Murcia

Cartagena

Granada

Malaga

Almeria

C. de Palos

PORTUGAL

Lisbon

Oporto

Seville

Cadiz

Gibralter

Straits of Gibraltar

Tangier

Larache

C. St. Vincent

THE MEDITERRANEAN

Algier

Tunis

PART OF AFRICA

Marocco

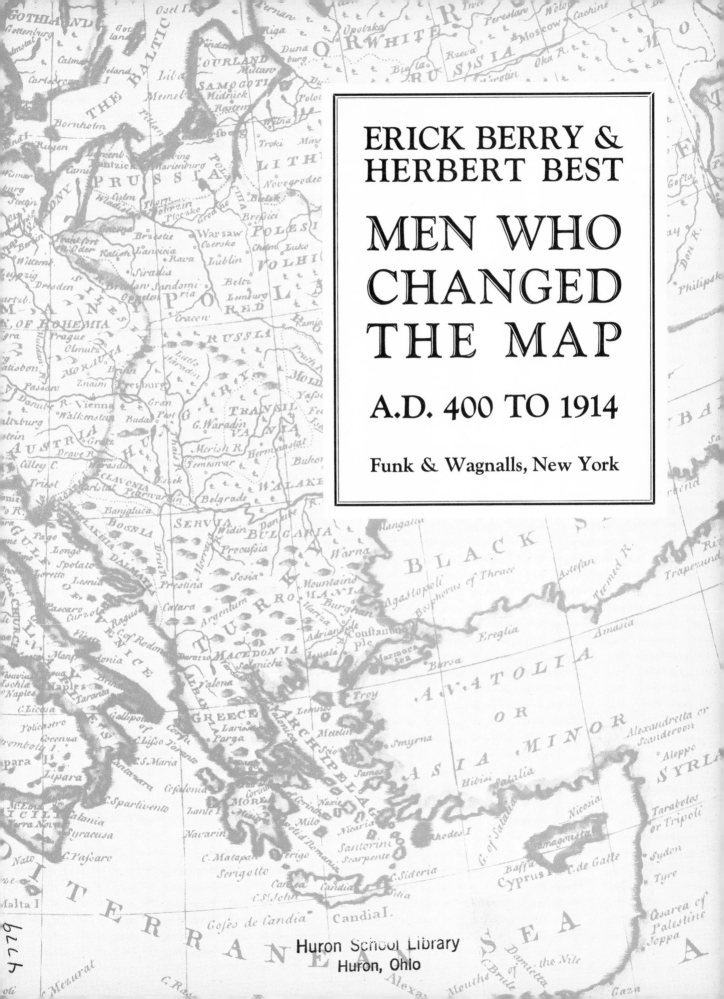

ERICK BERRY & HERBERT BEST

MEN WHO CHANGED THE MAP

A.D. 400 TO 1914

Funk & Wagnalls, New York

Huron School Library
Huron, Ohio

for Elizabeth Nichols,
who planted the seed

Text copyright © 1967 by Erick Berry and Herbert Best.
Maps copyright © 1967 by Laszlo Matulay.
Published in 1968 by Funk & Wagnalls,
A Division of Reader's Digest Books, Inc.
Library of Congress Catalog Card Number: 67-26044.
Printed in the United States of America.
First printing.

Picture research by Gale Sasson

MAPS BY LASZLO MATULAY

Photographs: Arab Information Center, New York City, 39;
The Bettmann Archive, 36, 37, 41, 43, 48, 50, 55, 60, 76, 78,
79, 81, 93, 100, 115, 124, 131, 138, 140, 143; Black Star, 71;
Brown Brothers, 16, 34, 77, 80; Culver Pictures, 6, 8; French
Embassy Press & Information Division, New York City,
51, 69, 148, 150, 152, 154, 156, 159; The Granger Collection,
52, 89, 126, 127, 133, 155, 160, 161; Hispanic Society of
America, 123, 132; The Metropolitan Museum of Art, 23,
(Bequest of Benjamin Altman) 110, (Anonymous Gift)
101, (The James F. Ballard Collection) 35, (Harris Bris-
bane Dick Fund) 49, 153, (Fletcher Fund) 21, 26, (Bequest
of Mary Martin) 142, (Gift of J. Pierpont Morgan) 9, 17,
18, 24, 29, (Gift of Giulia P. Morosini) 102, 117, (Bequest
of Alfred Duane Pell) 139 lower, (Bequest of George D.
Pratt) 109, (Rogers Fund) 91, 94, 103, 106, 139 above, 151,
(Bequest of George C. Stone) 104; The New York Public
Library Picture Collection, 3, 11, 40, 53, 54, 63, 67, 86, 87,
88, 90, 92, 95, 116, 122, 128, 141, 157; Rymer's *Foedera*, 65;
Smithsonian Institution, 107, 112; United Press Internation-
al, 64; *Vetusta Monumenta*, Society of Antiquaries of London, 61, 62.

Contents

Of Maps and Men

Maps, even today, need constant revision—and perhaps more today than ever. Dependent countries attain independence, other countries unite, and great nations swallow a part or a whole of smaller ones. New boundaries must be drawn in place of former ones, and new colors applied so that the changes are easily visible.

A comparison of old maps with those of today makes it clear that nations, often driven by the fortunes of war, have ebbed and flowed over the centuries like tides. Big nations have conquered smaller ones, but sometimes smaller ones have been the conquerors. Civilized peoples have resisted barbarians, but barbarians have often conquered the civilized.

It would be easy to attribute this ebb and flow to one cause—population explosion—but this would not be true in every case. A population may provide the pressure for national expansion, but it is the leader who directs the force and channels it to victory or who chooses the generals to command that force. Sometimes the leader even creates the force, uniting by conquest or treaty small and weak states until they can throw off the oppression of a far larger one.

The puzzle remains as to how this outstanding personality—the leader—achieves his purpose. In early days he had no organized government, no police or standing army to support him. He resembled a gang leader more than he did a president or king. He was a personal "boss," who retained his position, even his life, by rewarding and punishing as he saw fit. So long as he remained in authority, he had unlimited power of life and death over his lesser chiefs and everyone else in his domain. He was akin to, and sometimes even descended from, the paternal head of the clan who exercised complete control over his family. But this lasted only so long as he had the skill and power to enforce his will.

Sometimes, like the giant Viking chiefs, he owed his position to his prowess as a warrior in hand-to-hand combat. Sometimes he was an unscrupulous primitive politician, an efficient organizer, an able tactician, or, perhaps, any combination of these three. Competition was tough on the way up, but it was only after he had reached the top that his real troubles began. He had assumed the role of lion tamer over several hundred thousand unruly followers. They either obeyed him, or they killed him.

The leader had many dangerous rivals, men who would cut him down or poison him if they could. Daily he made more enemies by enforcing his orders; and whether those orders were good or bad made no difference—they had to be obeyed. In maintaining peace within his borders, he naturally aroused the resentment of his young warriors who felt they had honorable feuds to maintain, or wrongs to avenge.

Almost always the best solution to his problems was to lead his people into war. That was easy to arrange. A foreigner was always considered an enemy, one who spoke an odd and different language, looked different, dressed differently, had ridiculous customs, and could scarcely be thought of as human. To seize the foreigner's crops and women in a raid was legitimate hunting; to occupy his land and enslave him was still more profitable—and righteous.

Victory, even if the leader himself never smote with the sword or thrust with the spear, raised him to heroic stature. It made him semisacred, for success proved that he was favored by the god, or gods, or by the ancestors of his people. Early Norse chieftains, Pharaohs and Roman emperors were actually deified and worshiped. Even Christian kings became God's anointed: it was very convenient for a tribal chief to be sanctified and turned into a superhuman. A demigod was more likely to be obeyed, and to kill him was something more than common, everyday murder—it was sacrilege.

It is almost impossible, today, to imagine and feel the force of such hero worship. Combine the enthusiasm sports crowds feel for the champions of baseball, basketball, football, golf or boxing with the fervor aroused by a public orator or revivalist preacher and the hysteria stirred up by pop singers; temper this with the fear and respect inspired by the powerful ruler of a people; focus this upon just one man, the father figure of a multitude, and you begin to sense the awe and devotion that an Attila, an Alexander the Great, or a Caesar could inspire.

Such earthshakers show no common pattern. They are found among many different races; they were young or middle-aged, and even included some women. According to our standards they were good or evil, destructive or constructive, selfish or self-sacrificing. They had only a few traits in common, one of which was the possession of abnormal will power and self-confidence that resulted in an unshakable sense of purpose. Another was a more than man-sized personality. A third, which may be the result of combined purpose and personality, is what has recently come to be called *charisma*—the magic quality of leadership that makes one man believe, trust, and follow another to the death.

Such men—and women—were the leaders who made or erased whole nations, broke open the boundaries of mountain, deserts, and seas. They were the ones who changed our map. Tomorrow, unless human nature itself changes, such men will once more shake the earth.

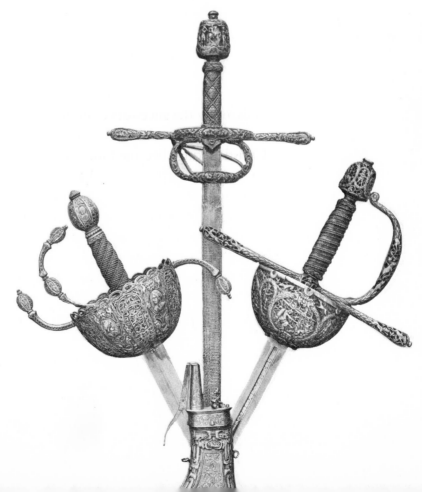

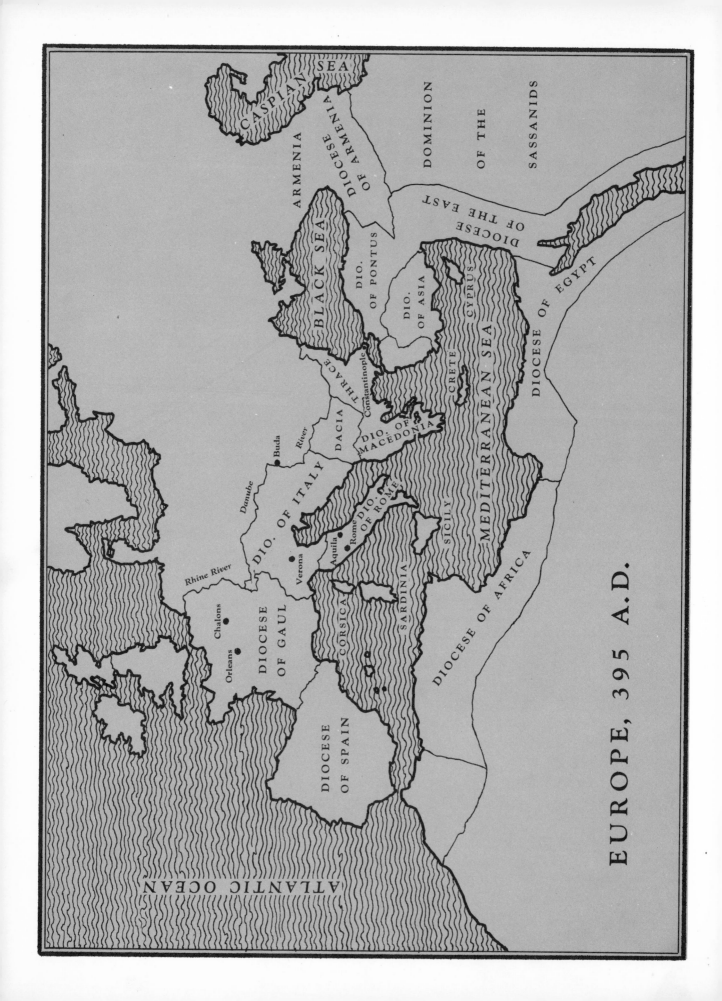

EUROPE, 395 A.D.

[? - 453]

Attila the Hun

The Huns were warlike nomads who for centuries had lived by conquest and pillaging in the plains below the Altai Mountains. It was against the Huns that the Chinese Emperor Hwang-te had built the Great Wall of China 258 years before Christ. Under Attila the Huns reached the peak of their power, terrorizing the peoples of both the Eastern and Western Roman Empire.

Their lives were wholly dedicated to war, and they were excellent fighters. But they could only fight on horseback. Unlike the Romans, they never mastered the art of attacking a fortified city; they had neither scaling ladders nor catapults. Their strength lay in the speed of their attack, their splendid marksmanship with spear and arrow, their fine horsemanship and superb horses (which were of a special breed and came from the mountains north of the plains). These stallions, whose strong backs and legs and hard hoofs allowed them to scramble over rocks and stony pastures, were far superior to the plains horses—and as the Huns did not shoe their mounts, such hard hoofs were especially valuable. Each year the tribes took their mares to the foothills where they mated with the mountain stallions, raising a more intelligent and stronger muscled strain than the small Mongol ponies. These Fergana horses, called "celestials" by the Chinese, allowed the Hun leaders to form a corps of heavily armed fighters, which worked alongside the lighter, faster corps.

Under the Khans (the princely leaders), the Huns gradually developed a semiunited state. Ruthlessly nibbling away at neighboring states, and always acquiring more grazing land, at the same time they attracted the best of the enemy warriors to join them. They did not cultivate the soil but kept constantly on the move, folding their tents, taking their women, camels, and ponies with them from

Attila the Hun, Scourge of God

waterhole to waterhole. A captured leader was usually beheaded; the warrior who captured him kept the skull as a drinking bowl and retained for his own use whatever booty he had taken.

Attila, their greatest leader, was described by a historian of his own day as "a man born into the world to shake nations." Most conquerors attain their goal as the result of a dedication that begins early in life. Attila was an exception. He was already in his middle years when he became the leader of a people whose sole ambition was war and among whom every man was a trained fighter. Thus, the tempting lands of the Eastern and Western empires lay spread out before him; his fighting force was at hand.

Rua, King of the Huns, died in 433 A.D. leaving his nephews Bleda and Attila as heirs to his throne. Bleda soon vanished, probably murdered by Attila. This left only Attila to maintain authority over a people who were on the one hand brave, but on the other cruel and treacherous. Marcellinus, a Gothic historian, describes the Huns as "having a shapeless lump, not a head, with pinholes rather than eyes." Their faces were fierce, he says, because they scarred the cheeks of males at birth and they "grow old beardless and their young men are without beauty because a face furrowed by the sword spoils by its scars the natural beauty of a beard." Marcellinus goes on to describe the Huns as "short in stature, quick in bodily movement, alert horsemen, broad shouldered, ready in the use of bow and arrow."

Attila, it is said, was a man who never laughed or smiled. He preferred plain food and avoided luxuries of all kinds. "He was haughty in his walk, rolling his eyes hither and thither, so that the power of his proud spirit showed even in the movement of his body." He was short and broad shouldered, with small eyes and a thin gray beard despite his facial scars; his dark complexion and flat nose were clear indications of his Mongolian origin.

Like many of the leaders of his day, Attila could neither read nor write; at that period such accomplishments were left to the scribes and the Christian monks. He had none of the civilization or religion of Rome or Constantinople. In fact, he seems to have despised them. But he ruled over a free and very proud people, who, in spite of the legends, were not very much more cruel or oppressive than those whom they fought for domination of Europe.

By the fourth century A.D. the Huns, moving ever westward, had established their seminomadic life south and west of the Danube River. The palace and main settlement were at a place called Etzelberg, where Buda now stands. This vast capital was probably more a military camp than a city. The palace, an enormous building of logs, was walled and floored with hewn planks, and its beams were of carved wood. Skins, wall hangings, and an open fire in the center of the room made it habitable. Outside the palace, the lesser chiefs lived in huts and tents with their followers and many wives.

The Huns had always dwelt in tents and had not acquired a taste for physical comfort; but they did have a never-ending craving for portable luxuries, such as gold and silver drinking cups and richly ornamented weapons. Since the Huns had few craftsmen, they could obtain such articles only from the spoils of war.

Early in the fourth century the Huns had migrated from a place in central Asia between the Lake of Aral and Lake Balkhash. Their westward movement had touched off other tribal migrations ahead of them. The Goths, who came from the north and had previously settled on the Vistula, had already moved down to an area north of the Black Sea. There, pushed on by the Huns, they moved again, this time into Thrace. Then Alaric, a Goth who had served the Huns as a general in the Roman army, decided to carve out his own kingdom. He marched his people, almost unopposed, into what is now Greece. There he halted for a few years to train his warriors. Finally, following the west coast of the Adriatic, he invaded Italy and sacked many cities, including Rome itself. After that, he continued down the toe of the Italian peninsula.

At about this time, another group—composed of the Vandals, Suivi and Alans—had swept down from the valley of the Elbe and reached as far as Florence. From northern Italy they burst through Burgundy with an army of 200,000 horsemen, crossed the Rhine and all but reached the English Channel. They sacked and burned the cities of Trier, Mainz, Rheims, Arras and Tournai, then crossed the Pyrenees and plundered Spain from north to south. But the

Goths drove them out of Spain and the Vandals and their allies crossed into North Africa and conquered it as far east as Carthage.

Thus, invasions by both Goths and Vandals had subjugated much of Europe and North Africa. And what others had done, Attila and his Huns could do. After all, it was the Huns who, a century before Attila, had defeated the Goths and driven many of them to seek the protection of the Roman Empire. Attila wished to match the earlier triumphs of the Huns and gain greater triumphs of his own. In any case, it is doubtful whether the leader had any choice but to fight, if he wished to satisfy his warlike subjects.

As a good general, he first made certain of his strength at home and subdued neighboring tribes to keep his men in training. By the year 441 Attila's army numbered 500,000 men, most of them horsemen. His first move was to invade the Roman provinces of Dacia, Macedonia, and Thrace, thus threatening the strong, walled city of Constantinople, capital of the Eastern Roman Empire.

In 441 and 442 Attila fought and won several battles with the army of the Emperor Theodosius II. In 442, Theodosius agreed to a truce, but he refused to turn over to Attila the fugitives of battle. So the war was renewed and again Attila forced the Emperor to sue for peace. This time Theodosius did agree to the terms: all fugitives would be handed over to Attila and the Emperor would pay a tribute of 2,100 pounds of gold per year, three times what he had previously

Mounted on their "celestials," the Huns terrorized the Roman Empire

agreed to pay. In the course of this campaign, the Huns sacked 70 towns and enslaved 2,000 men, women, and children. The Balkans, where most of the fighting went on, did not recover for four centuries.

With each long line of women captives, and each primitive wagon creaking with loot that appeared back in Attila's capital city, his hold over the unruly Huns became more secure. They had seen what their leader could accomplish for them. And now he thought it safe to start a more ambitious campaign to prove that he could equal the past achievements of Alaric the Goth. Having dealt with the Eastern Roman Empire, he could now turn his attention to the Western Empire. But he needed some excuse, no matter how slight, since Valentinian III, the Emperor of the West, continued to pay his tribute. He found his excuse in a clever way.

Valentinian's sister Honoria had been seduced by one of her chamberlains and was banished in disgrace to Constantinople. She sent a ring and a message to Attila, asking him to rescue her. He, however, chose to interpret her message as an offer of marriage. He now laid claim to her and to half of the Western Empire as her dowry. His claim was rejected, as he had no doubt expected, and he marched against Valentinian with his army.

Following the northern bank of the Danube, then striking across the Rhine, he invaded Gaul, one of the chief provinces of the Western Empire. It is said that he had agents everywhere, many of them members of the tribes against whom he made war. Their task was to undermine the morale of his enemies by spreading exaggerated accounts of the Huns' appalling cruelty. Attila proceeded westward, levelling the towns of Trier and Metz, massacring or enslaving their citizens. On he marched, sacking most of the towns in his path until he reached Orleans. He met with little opposition; his agents had done their work well.

The Roman Empire watched his advance with mounting terror. It was suffering from every known political disease—from corruption to downright treason. Its proud provinces, unwilling to accept Roman rule since the Roman legions could no longer protect them, were as much inclined to accept this new conqueror as to oppose

Silver spear ornament like those from the Western Roman Empire during the time of Attila

him. Such strength as the Western Empire possessed lay not with her own citizens, but with the barbarians within her borders.

The greatest of the barbarian chieftains was Theodoric, King of the Goths, who had settled near Toulouse. To stop Attila, Theodoric made a forced march north to meet the Huns, who had come from Thrace along the shores of the Mediterranean. Theodoric was joined by the Roman forces in Gaul and, with Franks from northern Gaul, led his men into battle at Chalons. This was to be one of the most important battles of the century; for the first time, the Romans and barbarians of the West united in a major effort to repel invaders from the East.

Attila, badly defeated in an attempt to take the city of Orleans, withdrew his army to the Campania—the open country to the northeast. He placed the main body of his troops in the Catalonian Plains at Chalons. There he was met by the Roman forces under the command of their ruler Aetius, and the Goths and their allies under the command of Theodoric. The battle began on June 20, 442. Attila charged directly into the center of the enemy force. There was fierce hand-to-hand fighting, during which the aged Theodoric fell from his horse and was trampled to death under the feet of his own men. By dawn of the next day, after a long night in which the armies fought each other in darkness, the Huns were in complete confusion. Attila retired to his camp with the remainder of his army, where he blockaded himself against attack. But his situation was desperate, for he had almost no food or supplies. The Romans and Goths laid seige to his camp and it seemed that he would have to kill himself or surrender. But Attila was saved by the political cunning of the Romans. Aetius, fearing that the Goths would become too strong if they no longer had to defend themselves against Attila, allowed the Hun leader to escape.

Thus, the Huns were still strong enough to threaten the Goths. But they were also strong enough to threaten the Romans. And a year after his escape from Chalons, Attila marched on Rome.

He crossed the Alps unopposed and attacked Aquelia. He was victorious. The town was so thoroughly destroyed that it was never rebuilt. The enemy fled before him, many taking refuge in the small fishing villages among the swamps and lagoons of what is now

Pope Leo I and Roman senators, at left, plead with Attila for peace

Venice. At Verona and Vicenza, Attila was more humane and allowed Pavia and Milan to purchase their safety by paying an enormous ransom. Attila halted at the river Po. Valentinian had fled to Rome, and the road to Rome was now open.

Pope Leo I and two senators hastened north from Rome to plead with the conqueror for peace. Leo the Great was a man of commanding personality, and tradition credits him with a miracle in that he was able to persuade Attila to withdraw. But it is doubtful that Attila, a complete heathen, was much impressed by the majesty of the Roman Pope. It is more likely that Attila withdrew in order to avoid the plague that had broken out in northern Italy and had already caused some losses among the Huns.

Back in his capital at Buda, Attila threatened to return to Rome the following spring unless Honoria, whom he still had not seen, was given to him in marriage. But in the meantime he consoled himself with another bride, a girl of his own people named Ildico. Though usually moderate, the Hun leader celebrated his marriage with plentiful food and wine. The next morning he was found dead in his bridal bed. Some claimed that his bride had given him poison.

Almost immediately after his death, Attila's empire broke apart. The Hun tribe, so varied and quarrelsome, had never really been consolidated into a nation. It was only the skill and authority of Attila that had held it together. Following Attila's death, several of the tribes under a leader named Ardaric staged a revolt against Attila's sons. Ellak, the eldest son, met the rebels near the river Nota in Pannonia and was slain, along with 30,000 of his warriors.

In twenty years as their ruler, Attila had for a short time united the warring tribes that made up the Huns. He had driven the Goths into the shelter of the Roman Empire and held both Eastern and Western empires at his mercy. Later, many legends grew up about Attila the Earth Shaker. The most important of these is told in the twelfth-century folk poem, the *Nibelungenlied*. In this poem, Attila is called Etzel, and Ildico is called Kriemhild. It is a wild, barbaric tale of magic, war, and vengeance, as fateful as a Greek tragedy.

Under Attila the Huns were the terror of Europe. But after his death they dispersed, some settling under Roman protection in Little Scythia and others in Serbia and Bulgaria. The rest returned to South Russia and their nomadic life.

TERRITORY RULED BY ATTILA, 450 A.D.

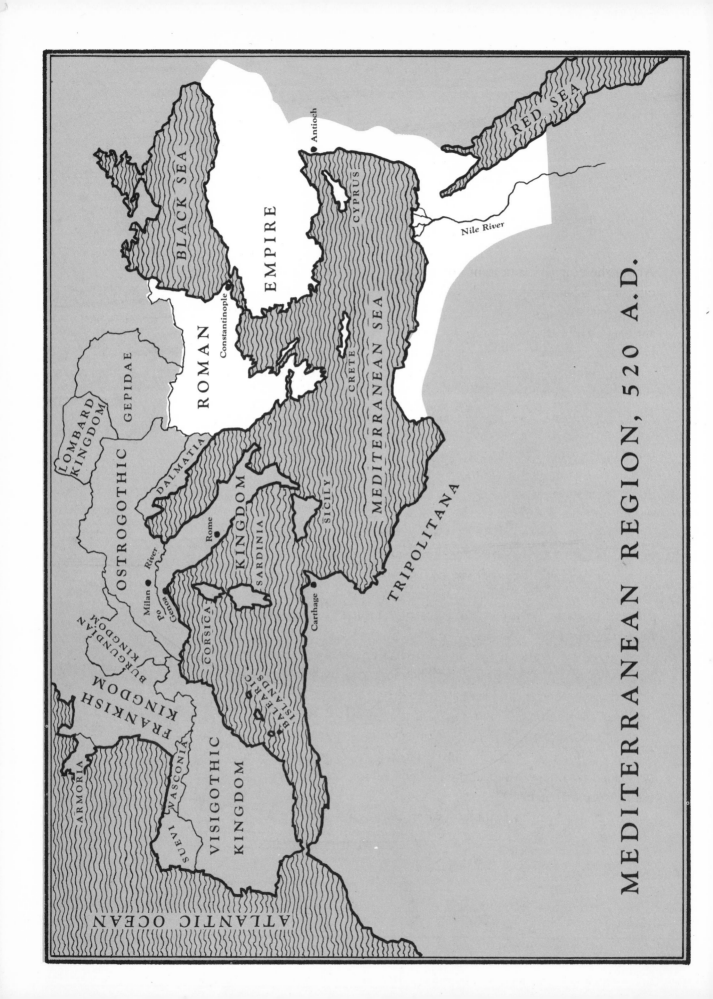

MEDITERRANEAN REGION, 520 A.D.

Justinian the Great

About the year 500, a peasant boy named Flavius rode into the great city of Constantinople to seek his fortune. He was a little above average height, of fair complexion, curly haired, with a pleasant manner and easy smile. He was born a Christian in 483 in the district of Dardania, probably of Slavonic parentage.

Constantinople, once called Byzantium, was the richest city in the world, the capital of what remained of the eastern half of the Roman Empire. The boy's uncle Justin, a tough old soldier who could neither read nor write, was commander of the Emperor's household guards. He adopted the youth and renamed him Justinian. Bright and ambitious, Justinian settled down to learn his way about in the complicated politics of the city and to develop abilities that would serve him well in his new home.

When the Emperor Anastasius died in 518, it was Justinian's good fortune that his uncle became Emperior Justin I, while the other candidates quarreled among themselves. Justinian then became Commander of the Imperial Guard, a senator, and behind-the-scenes adviser to his uncle. Thus, as time passed, Justinian became more and more powerful.

After some years, he fell in love with an actress twenty years younger than he. Her name was Theodora. She was the daughter of the bear keeper at the Hippodrome, the city circus, and had been on the stage since childhood. She was greatly admired as a comedienne and dancer, but her moral reputation was somewhat dubious. The law prohibited a senator from marrying an actress, but Justinian persuaded his uncle to repeal the law and in 523 Justinian and Theodora were married.

Justinian hoped to become Emperor after his uncle—a dazzling

Justinian the Great

ambition for an unwarlike young politician—and now he began to plan still further ahead and on a much larger scale.

Back in the year 330 the Roman Emperor Constantine had created a capital in the East, and on the foundations of the small town of Byzantium had built the great city which he renamed Constantinople. In the year 476 Romulus Augustus, the last emperor of the Western Roman Empire, was deposed. It was Justinian's ambition to reconquer Italy, Africa, and Spain, and unite Rome and Constantinople into what had once been the mighty Roman Empire.

Of course this would be incredibly difficult. Justinian could not appeal to the patriotism of Ancient Rome, for the Eastern Empire was a mixture of races with scarcely a drop of Roman blood. Nor could he appeal to a common religious bond, since there was much hatred between the Christians of the West, whose allegiance was with Rome, and those Christians of the East who were loyal to Constantinople. Thus, because of these difficulties he would need to conquer Italy, and here lay another obstacle to success. Though

Commander of the Imperial Guard, Justinian had never drawn a sword or heard the whine of an enemy arrow. He was a politician and a student of theology, and could never become a popular military hero.

His first step—which seemed an easy one—was to persuade his uncle, the Emperor, to call a council to settle the religious differences between Rome and Constantinople. The council was a complete failure. Justinian next tried to unite the Eastern Empire in one religion. Here at home, he could and did use force, cruelly persecuting those Christian sects that did not agree with the doctrines of the official Orthodox Church. Among them was the sect of Monophysites who were well organized in Syria, Palestine, and Egypt, and had a powerful following in Constantinople itself. But Justinian's policy of enforced religious unity was not very successful and caused dangerous discontent.

In the year 527 the aging Justin officially appointed Justinian his co-ruler, and Justinian and Theodora were crowned with full honors as Emperor and Empress. Justin's death a few months later made them rulers in fact.

The new sovereign then took a puzzling step, and surely a risky one: he intentionally did all he could to make Theodora independent of him. In addition to the jewels and wealth that were hers as Empress, he granted her large country estates, built her a separate palace, and left her free to run her own life as she wished. The child actress, who had lived by her wits, charm, and courage from Constantinople to Egypt and back as a circus performer, was now every inch an Empress and a more respectable Empress than most. Her character was in many ways the opposite of her husband's. He was easygoing, friendly, and forgiving; she was now formal in manner and harshly unforgiving to her enemies. He tended to hatch elaborate long-term schemes which were often unrealistic; she was swift to seize an opportunity or to revise her plans to suit changing conditions. Moreover, Justinian was an Orthodox Catholic; Theodora was almost certainly a believer in the forbidden Monophysite heresy.

In other words, the beautiful Theodora had the very qualities that the new Emperor realized he lacked, and in setting her up in a

Gold necklace comes from 6th-century Byzantine Empire

separate establishment he could use her as a Minister of State in charge of Intelligence. People who dared not approach the Imperial Palace would feel free to talk with her, and her link with the dangerous Monophysites might be particularly valuable. On occasion she was to oppose his plans, but on the whole she used her extraordinary powers with discretion. The painfully acquired knowledge of her underworld childhood allowed her to keep the brooding, fasting scholarly Emperor in touch with reality. Reputedly, with her cutthroats and prison cells in her palace (for personal enemies), she was certainly a realist.

When Justinian began to relax his persecution of heretics, the subtle influence of Theodora surfaced. The persecution had been as dangerous as it had been ineffective, and an assassination plot was being hatched in Constantinople about which Theodora and her agents must have heard rumors.

Justinian continued to seek unity through religion, but had no luck in persuading the Catholic and Orthodox factions to settle their differences. Then he tried another approach. Perhaps the Eastern and the remains of the Western Empire could be drawn together by another of Rome's ancient glories, even older than Christianity—the Roman Law. The Emperor appointed a committee with authority to collect all legal writings throughout the country, and turn all past legislation into one single code of law. It was a very sensible idea, for the mass of judicial decisions and Imperial decrees had grown so vast and complex that no one could understand them.

Meanwhile, around the year 530, Constantinople was threatened by the Persian Empire on the east, under a king named Chosroës. There had been numerous frontier incidents and both sides had fortified their small border towns against raiders. Seeing that the Persians were growing more active, the Emperor looked for a suitable man to lead his army. He chose Belisarius, a young but very skilled general, to take command.

Pearls and sapphires adorn gold bracelets
from the time of Justinian

JUSTINIAN THE GREAT   19

The Persians, with a force twice the size of Belisarius', advanced on the frontier town of Daras. Instead of letting himself be besieged, Belisarius met the enemy outside the town walls. The Persians drove back Belisarius' right flank, but a small group of cavalry hidden behind a hillock cut into the enemy's undefended left flank. Both movements left openings in the Persian line of battle, and into these Belisarius threw his main force. The Persians broke and fled, leaving 5,000 dead.

Next, the general faced a large Persian raid under an Arab named Mundhir who, by cutting across the Arabian desert, had by-passed the frontier defenses and almost reached Antioch, the second city of the Empire. By forced marches Belisarius threw his army of 20,000 between the Persians and Antioch. Mundhir retreated toward the desert. Belisarius was content to play wolf and sheep, cutting off strays from the Persian army. He knew that his men were unfit for the strain of a decisive battle, for all were weary from the forced march and a number were observing the Easter fast. Unfortunately, he was overruled by his army and the Battle of Callinicum that ensued was a disaster for his troops, many of whom deserted.

Belisarius was recalled to Constantinople to face an inquiry but was exonerated and ordered to form a new army. To prevent it from taking control again, he raised a small body of personal guards, the famous *Comitatus* (Companions). Paid by him and obedient to him only, they formed a hard core of veterans inside the main force.

Meanwhile, trouble was brewing in Constantinople. Fiscal abuses and religious issues helped to divide political groups. The four main parties, Blues, Greens, Reds, and Whites took their names from the colors worn by their chariot drivers in the Hippodrome. Like gangsters, the groups murdered members of opposing groups and protected themselves by force or political influence. The Orthodox Blues hated and were hated by the Monophysite Greens.

The trouble started at the Sunday races. A professional demagogue, his voice trained to carry across the 20,000 spectators, heckled the Emperor in his royal box and provoked a fight between the Blues and the Greens. Five of the rioters were hanged, but two of them, one a Green and one a Blue, survived the hanging and took sanctuary in a church. At a later race meeting, the Greens demanded that the member of their group who had escaped hanging should be freed. Justinian refused. The Greens then appealed to the Blues, who also wanted to protect the fugitive member of their group. So the two parties, though enemies of long standing, united against the Emperor. The danger point had been reached.

The combined mob of Blues and Greens surged out of the Hippodrome, made for the City Hall, and released all prisoners; they beat the officials and burned the place down. Next the Senate House and the Cathedral of Hagia Sophia went up in flames. Finally, the mob set fire to the entrance of the Imperial Palace; inside were Justinian, Theodora, and the ministers of state.

The next day three ministers entered the royal box (by the private entrance from the Palace) and tried to calm the mob. The demands hurled back at them made it clear that the riot had become a revolt, organized to replace Justinian on the throne by a relative of Anastasius, the former Monophysite Emperor. During the following days Belisarius and his general, Mundus, led their bodyguards against the rioters in the streets, while more of the city went up in flames. On the following Sunday Justinian again entered his royal box and after a useless appeal to his people returned to the Palace.

The situation remained critical. Justinian was advised by his ministers to leave the city. Theodora opposed the move, declaring that she would remain, as she preferred to be buried in the royal purple of an Empress rather than the white shroud of a commoner. Belisarius and Mundus made another sortie with their men. The streets were deserted, so they made their way to the Hippodrome. Though armed, the spectators were too tightly packed to defend themselves and 30,000 were slaughtered. The revolt was ended.

In 533, the Persians at last agreed to a treaty of peace. Now Justinian felt free to turn his eyes to Italy, though he could do nothing in that direction so long as the Vandals of North Africa held the Mediterranean with their fleet. Two years earlier the Vandals had deposed and imprisoned their ruler who had been on friendly terms with Constantinople. This would serve as a good excuse for Justinian to declare war—if he dared.

Empress Theodora is shown at center in this copy of a mosaic completed between the years 536 and 547 in Ravenna, Italy

The wars of earlier Emperors against the Vandals had been disastrous. Also, wars always meant additional taxation. So both the populace and his own advisers were opposed to Justinian's plan. He knew that his throne was at stake and took every precaution that money and diplomacy could provide.

In June, 533, Belisarius and his new wife Antonia set sail for Sicily with 16,000 highly trained soldiers, 20,000 sailors, and 500 ships. Justinian had prepared the Goths, and the fleet was welcomed. There Belisarius heard the good news that the Vandal fleet was engaged in subduing Sardinia. He made straight for Tripolitania in North Africa and landed without opposition, for Justinian's diplomacy had made the people friendly. Belisarius' organization and discipline were so precise that the whole army, including his 5,000 cavalry archers with their horses, was able to march westward only two days after landing.

Eleven days later the Vandal army near Tunis mistimed a complicated three-pronged attack and was defeated with heavy losses by Belisarius. The Emperor's skillful diplomacy made Belisarius welcome in the rich city of Carthage, and his fleet sailed into the bay unopposed. Strict orders against looting helped to establish good relations with neighboring tribes. Everything had gone according to the Emperor's plan.

Now the Vandal fleet returned from Sardinia, and its fighting men reinforced the Vandal army, which advanced from the west to within 20 miles of Carthage. Belisarius' cavalry made feint attacks on the enemy, then retreated to draw them in pursuit. The cavalry archers then shot up the pursuers, killing 800 and losing only 50 of their own men. Belisarius brought up his infantry and the Vandals broke and fled. A few days later another advance captured the Vandals' hoard of gold. In March the Vandal king surrendered.

Later, in the year 534, Belisarius declined Justinian's offered appointment as Governor of North Africa, and sailed with the Vandal king and the Vandal gold to Constantinople. The gold had repaid the Imperial Treasury for the cost of the war (which had been a brilliant and unexpected success), the Orthodox Christian faith had been imposed on the heretical North Africans, the Vandal fleet

The Cathedral of Hagia Sophia in Constantinople, rebuilt by Justinian

could no longer control the eastern Mediterranean, and Justinian could sail his army to Italy whenever he chose. The grateful Emperor granted his successful general a triumphal procession amid a rejoicing populace.

Without stirring from Constantinople, Justinian had busied himself with the kind of work he did best. The ashes of Hagia Sophia (destroyed during the revolt) were scarcely cold before he summoned two great architects, Anthemios and Isodoros, and set them to rebuilding the cathedral, offering them all the resources of the Empire. The style of architecture and decoration they developed for the new cathedral was to influence all of Europe. The mosaics

—pictures formed of small pieces of stone, ceramic, and precious metals—were the finest in the world. The stained-glass windows, inspired by Persia and the Orient, became a feature of European churches for centuries to come. Byzantine embroidered fabrics, stiff with gold and gems, were later adopted by the court of Charlemagne and became the standard for church vestments in the West as well as the East.

Justinian built many other churches and palaces, but none so famous as Hagia Sophia; it was completed in five years and ten months by 10,000 workmen. The rebuilding of the cathedral was a clear sign that Justinian intended Constantinople, not Rome, to be the capital of the combined Eastern and Western Empire he planned.

His work on Roman Law had made steady progress, even during the Blue-Green revolt. By 529 the *Code of Civil Law*, or Justinian Code, was completed and made public. This massive but poorly organized collection of laws (in more than 60 volumes) was a magnificent piece of work. But it reflected the underlying barbarity of its age. Though the status of women, children, and slaves was somewhat improved, vicious punishments were prescribed for pagans and Christian heretics. The punishments ranged from fines to flogging, mutilation, beheading, crucifixion, and burning alive. Imprisonment was not imposed as punishment, but only used to hold an offender awaiting trial.

The *Code* summarized what we would call written law. The committee was now set to work codifying earlier court decisions and, by 533, had produced a *Digest* of judicial decisions and interpretations by noted lawyers. The committee's final product was the *Institutions*, an elementary textbood for students of law. While the whole body of *Code*, *Digest*, and *Institutions* had profound effects upon the development of European law, it is the elementary *Institutions* that cast a clear light on the basic ideal of Roman Law: the principle of justice, an abstract and possibly unattainable ideal. The principle dates back to the Roman Twelve Tables of 450 B.C. that required a citizen "To live uprightly. To harm none. To give everyone his due ['Sum cuique tribuere']." For the preservation of this ideal, we have the *Institutions* to thank.

Gold cup with hammered designs comes from Byzantine civilization centered in Albania

Thanks to Belisarius and his own careful preparations, Justinian was now free to take another gamble in the west. The opportunity came, and at the right time.

Italy had been ruled by the Ostrogoths since 493. During this time the Pope had held only religious authority over the Italians. Justinian needed a pretext to fight the Goths. It conveniently happened that Amalasuntha, the rightful Queen of the Goths, had been imprisoned by her husband and now appealed to Justinian for protection. Justinian invited her to come to Constantinople as his honored guest; but by the same messenger Theodora sent very different instructions—that Amalasuntha must be disposed of. Did Theodora double-cross Justinian because she was afraid of receiving a younger, better-bred, and equally beautiful and intelligent rival in her husband's court? Or did she take this step with Justinian's connivance? Whatever the motive, the desired result was achieved. The Queen of the Goths was strangled in her bath, and Justinian declared war.

At the end of 535, Belisarius sailed for Sicily with his army. The Goths in Sicily were now enemies, but offered little opposition, and in the following year he crossed to the mainland of Italy and captured Naples. The next year he took Rome, without opposition; but the Goths struck down from the north in greater force and besieged him.

Again Belisarius showed himself a brilliant and unconventional tactician, but he had too few troops to hold what he had gained. War raged up and down Italy. Cities were captured and recaptured, and citizens were butchered or carried off into captivity. The Franks crossed the Alps, took towns, butchered all the Italian inhabitants, and looted and enslaved as far as Genoa. Yet, by masterly maneuvers and hard personal fighting, and using his wonderful *Comitatus* at the core of his disciplined army, by the year 539 Belisarius had driven the Goths back to Ravenna, their capital in the northeast.

But meanwhile Justinian was in trouble. North of Constantinople the Huns had invaded Illyria, enslaving 120,000 women and children and slaughtering the men. To the east and south the uneasy peace with Persia had ended. Chosroës, the Persian King, had seized the opportunity, while many of Justinian's men were in Italy, to capture

Justinian and members of court are shown in panel from Ravenna mosaic

the famous city of Antioch and kill the inhabitants. Then he cut through Syria to bathe in the Mediterranean. Satisfied by this exhibition of power he started for home with a long string of captives who were destined for slavery.

Justinian needed to recall his troops from Italy to oppose the Huns and the Persians. So he offered the Goths, whom Belisarius had bottled up in Ravenna, very generous terms of peace. They could keep the north of Italy beyond the Padus (Po) River, while the remainder of the country would be ruled as a province of Constantinople. Justinian's plan was to leave the Goths as a buffer state between the troublesome Franks (from across the Alps) and the remainder of Italy. This would free most of his troops to come home.

But Belisarius, who knew little of Justinian's wider problem, was appalled by the feebleness of the peace terms; he had only to capture Ravenna to end the war. Even the Goths were surprised, and asked Belisarius to give his personal guarantee that the terms were not a trick. He refused. So great was Belisarius' reputation that the King of the Goths offered to abdicate and make him King. Belisarius was allowed to enter Ravenna with his *Comitatus* as though to receive the crown. By treachery, he captured the King of the Goths, and the Gothic hoard of gold, and with these sailed home. The moment he left, war broke out again.

Having ruined Justinian's long-term plan, Belisarius received a poor welcome and no official triumph. Early in 541 he was sent hastily to the eastern front to work his usual tactical miracles. By the spring of the next year the Persians again threatened the eastern front of the Empire. Belisarius confronted the approaching Persian army which greatly outnumbered his forces. Chosroës retreated without fighting.

The cause of the Persian retreat may have been the bubonic plague, which was spreading throughout the Empire. Traveling slowly, the deadly plague reached Constantinople in 543, killing upwards of 250,000 in the city alone; it did not spare the Emperor himself. While Justinian lay at the point of death, gossip turned to whether Theodora would succeed him. Belisarius' officers, with time on their hands, were outspoken in their dislike of being commanded by a woman. Since Theodora was acting for Justinian, Bouzes, one of Belisarius' generals, was relieved of his command and ordered to Constantinople. Belisarius was placed under arrest, his *Comitatus* dispersed, and his fortune seized. Bouzes vanished, and two years later emerged, a wreck of a man, from solitary confinement in an airless underground cell in Theodora's palace. Fortunately, the successful commander in Africa and Italy was too valuable on the eastern front, and too trusted by Justinian, to be treated so drastically.

The Emperor recovered to find his grand design in ruins. Though Chosroës' army had also been struck by the plague, it was only temporarily out of action. Theodora had managed to depose John, Justinian's honest and efficient treasurer and tax collector, and had also ruined Belisarius, one of history's greatest generals. The Imperial Treasury was empty—the plague had reduced tax revenue to a mere dribble. And in Italy the situation was worse than ever.

Belisarius had to show his loyalty by reconquering Italy. Two-thirds of his private fortune was returned to him by the grudging and vindictive Theodora. He was sent off without his *Comitatus*, with only a junior rank and a miserable little army of 5,000. There was even a proviso that he must make Italy pay his men and could expect no help from the Imperial Treasury.

Belisarius could no longer go by sea, but had to march the long way around by Dalmatia (now part of Yugoslavia), for the Goths held central Italy and had a small fleet. With part of his small force he struck south and strengthened the defenses of Otranto on the heel of Italy, since that port would be essential later on. Rome was once more under siege by the Goths. His failure to relieve the city was the one blot on his career, for at a critical moment he turned back to rescue his wife Antonia, whom he mistakenly believed to be in danger.

The miserable war continued as before. With only a handful of new *Comitatus*, with troops who could seldom be paid and who, when captured, defected to the enemy, Belisarius, for all his hard fighting and skillful tactics, was unable to gain a decisive victory.

After four years, unable to get reinforcements from Justinian—who was engaged in pointless theological disputes—Belisarius came to a bitter decision. He swallowed his pride and sent Antonia to plead with Theodora, but the Empress had just died. Antonia, getting no help from Justinian, offered Belisarius' resignation. It was accepted, and the general returned to Constantinople.

He had scarcely arrived before he was accused of a plot to depose the now useless Justinian and place Germanus, the Emperor's popular nephew, on the throne. Belisarius was found innocent, and the other accused were pardoned. But the Emperor felt it wise to get Germanus out of the way, and sent him to command the troops in Italy.

Probably the new commander in chief planned to make himself an independent Emperor of Rome, for he married the heir to the Gothic throne and invested his fortune in a fine new army. But he had first to repel a new invasion of Illyria, and in this campaign he caught fever in the swamps and died.

Justinian tried again. He sent his old favorite Narses to Italy with 25,000 troops instead of the 5,000 that Belisarius had been allowed. Narses was now 75 years of age, and also a civilian at heart, but he had learned his tactics under Belisarius. For a year he steadily defeated the Goths, then turned his attention to the invading Franks. By 554, Italy was at last conquered and at peace. Narses, as the new Governor, administered the shattered country for the next three years.

Belisarius had one more moment of glory. Illyria had been invaded again, almost to the walls of Constantinople. The once famous general, now a private citizen, gathered a force of 500 soldiers and a larger number of untrained and ill-armed volunteers. The odds against him were overwhelming, but after a brief fight and the feint of a flanking movement, he repelled the invading Huns.

Justinian died in 565, having added North Africa, part of Spain, and Italy to his Empire. The peasant boy had come a long way, but his dream of uniting the two great Roman Empires had faded. (Since the death of Theodora in 548, he is said to have neglected his duties and devoted himself to monklike meditations and theological discussions.)

Today his fame rests on the accomplishments of his carefully chosen agents: on Anthemios who rebuilt Hagia Sophia to the Emperor's lasting glory; on Tribonian and his lawyers who produced

Gold pectoral ornament from 6th-century Byzantine Empire

the *Code*, the *Digest* and the *Institutions;* on John the Treasurer who found means to finance the Emperor's costly enterprises; and not the least on the marvelous general, the ever loyal Belisarius.

But more remarkable than any of these was Theodora, the child actress, daughter of the Hippodrome bearkeeper. She demanded marriage, though a law had to be revoked to make this possible. She showed her power by exacting full rights as an Empress and by demanding more freedom than any Empress was permitted. She showed her courage in refusing to allow Justinian and his ministers to flee from the Blue-Green revolutionaries. She showed her caution in having the Queen of the Goths murdered as a possible rival. And she showed her vindictiveness by exiling for life the irreplaceable John the Treasurer, whom she considered her enemy. To improve her prospects of becoming sole ruler she attempted to destroy Belisarius, and, after Justinian's recovery from the plague, refused to allow the general to be restored to full power. Instead, she made sure that he was sent off to Italy so handicapped that his failure was guaranteed.

After the death of Theodora, Justinian seems to have lost all grasp of public affairs, to have become a gloomy shadow of his former self. But what was his former self? His early accomplishments —gradually accruing power until he had replaced his uncle as Emperor, choosing the young Belisarius to carry out his military plans, and establishing Theodora as a power in herself—indicate a great degree of political skill. His later career is something else. If we subtract from the history of his reign the works of Theodora, Belisarius, Narses, John the Treasurer, and the others who carried out the Emperor's grand schemes, it is hard to find a man inside the Imperial robes. Instead we find an ambitious young peasant who became a crafty politician, a man who could not carry out his ambitious plans but knew how to choose subordinates who could. His personal character is even harder to understand. He was a man who fought to attain the Imperial purple, but later donned the robes of a monk; a strict moralist perhaps corrupted by his sophisticated young wife; a paradoxical man, perhaps as puzzling to himself as he is to us.

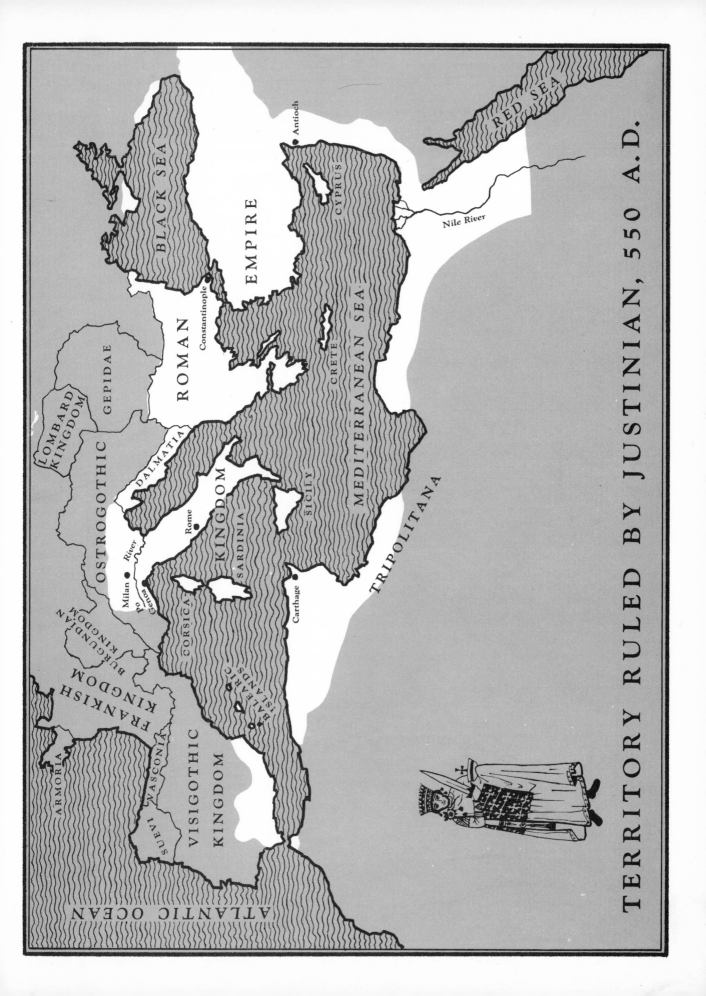

TERRITORY RULED BY JUSTINIAN, 550 A.D.

RED SEA

Antioch

CYPRUS

Nile River

BLACK SEA

EMPIRE

ROMAN

Constantinople

CRETE

MEDITERRANEAN SEA

GEPIDAE

LOMBARD
KINGDOM

OSTROGOTHIC

DALMATIA

KINGDOM

SICILY

TRIPOLITANA

Rome

SARDINIA

Milan

Po River

Genoa

CORSICA

Carthage

BURGUNDIAN
KINGDOM

FRANKISH

KINGDOM

BALEARIC
ISLANDS

ARMORIA

VASCONIA

SUEVI

VISIGOTHIC

KINGDOM

ATLANTIC OCEAN

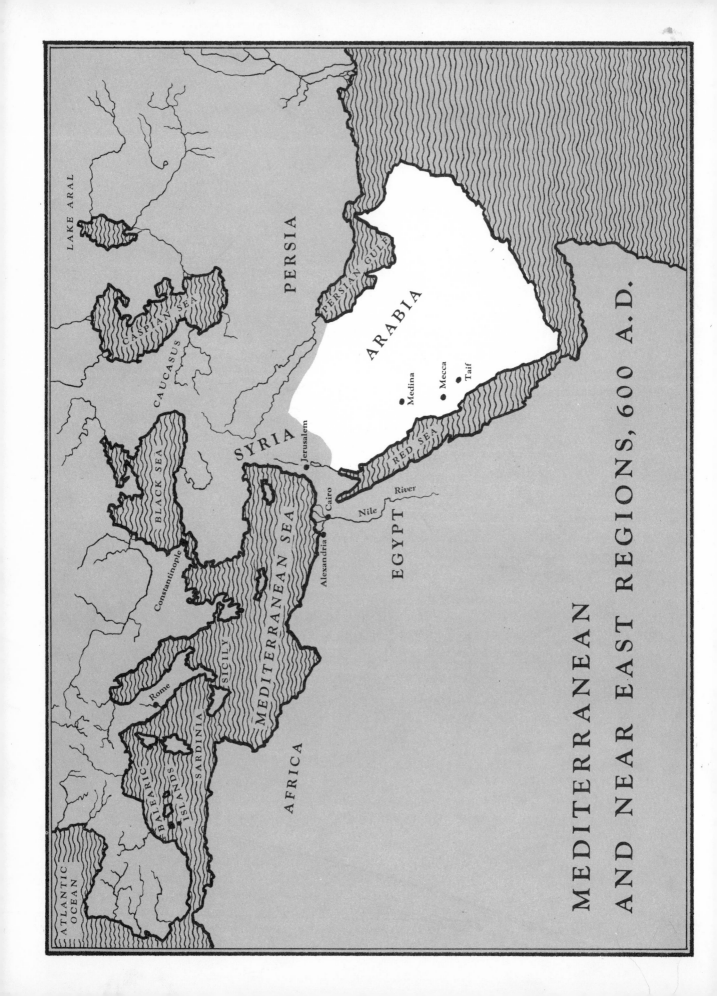

LAKE ARAL

CASPIAN SEA

CAUCASUS

PERSIA

PERSIAN GULF

ARABIA

• Medina

• Mecca

• Taif

BLACK SEA

SYRIA

Jerusalem •

RED SEA

River

Constantinople

Cairo •

Nile

EGYPT

Alexandria •

MEDITERRANEAN SEA

Rome •

SICILY

AFRICA

SARDINIA

BALEARIC ISLANDS

ATLANTIC OCEAN

MEDITERRANEAN
AND NEAR EAST REGIONS, 600 A.D.

Mohammed

At 40 years of age, Mohammed was an undistinguished Arab, a member of a respectable but poor family. His home was in the small town of Mecca, perched among scorching, barren hills and surrounded by desert. His father Abdullah had died before Mohammed was born, leaving his heirs five camels, a few goats, a small house of sunbaked brick, and a slave girl named Halimah.

When Mohammed was six years old, his mother died, and Halimah took care of him. Later he lived with his grandfather, Abd al-Mutallib, and then with his uncle, Abu Talib, who took him on trading expeditions across the desert. After Mohammed learned about the caravan trade from his uncle, he went to work as a camel driver for Khadijah, a widowed merchant woman. At the age of 25, he married this widow, who was 15 years older than he.

Since we know nothing about Mohammed's middle years, we can assume that he did nothing very remarkable for a man of his class and education. The tribe of Koreish ruled the town, and Mohammed, though he had relatives among the more important Koreish, belonged to the Hashimites, an unimportant subdivision of the Koreish. As was usual for boys of his time, Mohammed could neither read nor write, but he was still able to help his wife in her trading.

Mecca was one of three small stopping places in the western Arabian Desert through which meandered the long, slow caravans of camels from Egypt and Syria on their way to far-off India. Its main importance was as a religious center of the Arab tribes, whose varied idols were kept in the Kaaba (or Cube—so called because of its shape). Here in Mecca he met Christian and Jewish merchants who stayed in the town of mud and walled houses or in caravanseries, camp lodgings that were provided for the profitable pilgrim trade.

Mohammed, The Praised

An ordinary middle-aged man in turban and embroidered robe, who padded barefoot through the narrow, sandy streets, Mohammed was of average height. Unlike the sun-scorched desert dwellers, he was fair-skinned with flashing dark eyes and well-kept hair and beard —a typical Meccan. We do not know which of the tribal idols he worshiped, but it may have been the Black Stone, for later he preserved it. The ruling Koreish tribe, who were also the guardians of the Kaaba, had singled out one of the gods, called Allah, as the chief deity and patron of the city. This was the name Mohammed was to give to the One and Only God.

Mohammed may have been something of a freethinker, for he learned a little of the Christian religion and much of the Jewish, either from his fellow traders or from people he met on the expeditions of his youth. An activity that set this average-looking man apart from his neighbors was his unusual habit of withdrawing to a cave in the hills three miles outside the town to fast and meditate.

Once there had been several small kingdoms on the northwest of the arid desert, such as Saba, from which the Queen of Sheba went to visit Solomon. But by Mohammed's time no trace of these remained. Perhaps the climate had grown drier, forcing the inhabitants to move on to more fertile ground.

Throughout the desert, only one Arab in twelve was a townsman, and only one in twelve was a villager, living on the dates, vegetables and goats that he raised. Ten out of twelve were members of the nomadic Bedouin tribes, drifting from waterhole to waterhole and pasture to pasture to find water and grazing land for their goats, camels, and horses. These wandering tribes were like large families, each loosely organized under its paternal sheikh. The Bedouin tribes continually fought among themselves for water and grazing land, and raided one another again and again for women and camels. If a tribe was defeated, it would return later for revenge. The heavy death toll caused by this constant fighting was almost a blessing, for it checked overpopulation and, hence, starvation. A few tribes were lucky enough to be on the trade routes, where they could sell camels to the caravans, levy tolls, and sometimes rob and massacre them.

The few small cities which did exist had developed very little beyond the Bedouin system of tribal rule and tribal custom. These cities were able to defend themselves against raiders but were too weak to carry offensive warfare into the desert. The villagers, often liberated or runaway slaves, were neither rich nor warlike and were universally despised by the Bedouins. There seemed no common ground on which these mutually hostile groups could be joined into a nation. Mohammed was to find one—a common religious faith.

Moslem prayer rug made of silk and wool comes from Turkey

The inspiration came to him when he was 40 years of age. He was fasting and alone in the cave on Mount Hira when he fell asleep and saw a vision. The Archangel Gabriel (a figure in Jewish and Christian Scriptures but totally unconnected with any Arab deity) appeared to him and announced, "O Mohammed, you are the messenger of Allah." Since Allah was one of the gods of the Kaaba, the new religion was, from the first, a fusion of many older beliefs, and was to continue as such.

After receiving the vision and accepting Gabriel's words, Mohammed began to preach. At first he was mocked by the Koreish.

Then he began to make converts among the idolaters who came to pray at the Kaaba. But the merchants, whose livelihood depended on trade with the pilgrims coming to Mecca to worship the idols, became angry. The Prophet was forced to leave his home, and for two years he lived in the Hashimite quarter of the city. Then Abu Talib, his powerful protector, and his wife Khadijah, who had been his first convert, died. Mohammed sought refuge in Taif, a city 60 miles from Mecca, but the people of Taif drove him out.

He returned to Mecca and took a new wife. Her name was Ayesha, the daughter of one of his early converts, Abu Bekr. He soon made more converts in Mecca, among them several pilgrims from Medina. When these new converts turned to Medina, they sent a deputation to Mohammed begging him to come and preach in their city. Medina and Mecca were rival cities. Medina was situated in a fertile oasis, while Mecca had little but the pilgrim trade to support it. The rulers of Mecca considered Mohammed a troublemaker. Before long, they had had enough of him and ordered him killed.

The Prophet went into hiding. Some 200 Meccan converts made their way to Medina, and Mohammed soon followed them. He

The Archangel Gabriel appeared to Mohammed and named him the 'messenger' of Allah. Mohammed soon fled his native city

Mohammed arrives in Medina in 622 and is welcomed by his converts

was warmly received at the city gates. His journey from Mecca to Medina is known as the Hegira, or Flight, of September 24, 622, and is considered the turning point in Moslem history, for now the fugitive had become a leader. Shortly after arriving in Medina he began to announce the rules of his religion and to organize followers.

After the barren hills of Mecca, Medina must have seemed charming, with its groves of date palms, gardens, and small farms.

Medina was not a center of idol worship and had no pilgrim trade to protect; it could afford to be tolerant of the new preacher. Both Jewish and Christian sects regarded him with approval at first and found much in common with the new religion. Its basic rules were simple. They required three private prayers a day and, at first, bowing toward Jerusalem. Later this rule would be changed, and the Faithful would bow toward Mecca, the city of the Prophet's birth.

In Medina, Mohammed established his first mosque (Masjid, the "place to bow down and worship"). The mosque's first service was held to celebrate the oath of brotherhood he had imposed upon both Medinan and Meccan converts. The service opened as all Moslem services have opened since then. All the worshippers repeated the phrase, "Allah is most great!" Then they bowed in prayer three times to indicate their submission to Allah in the age-old form of physical surrender to a conqueror. Mohammed used the sermon that followed to announce new revelations and proclaim them as law. This simple

Moslems in many lands offer prayers and worship to Allah inside mosques like this one in the city of Cairo

ceremony, without priests or sacrifices, remains the pattern for the prayers of countless millions of Moslems to this day.

Mohammed had passed from enquirer to believer to preacher. Now he had to take command. The homeless immigrants from Mecca were his first problem. Every square foot of the Medina oasis was jealously guarded, for beyond it lay nothing but desert, from which the small tribes could scrape a living, but in which city folk would starve.

In 623, Mohammed, then 53 years of age and a merchant with no previous record of fighting, personally led an attack on a large caravan headed from Syria to Mecca. Meccans came out to defend the caravan but were routed. Some of the prisoners were put to death. Others were held for ransom. The booty of the caravan was rich indeed.

One-fifth of the loot went to Mohammed for religious and charitable purposes. (Early Moslems, like early Christians, included a large number of slaves and poor people, who had no means of support.) Mohammed's teachings made alms-giving a religious duty for the well-to-do. The Koran, which Mohammed had already begun to dictate to a scribe, was definitely a poor man's Bible, stating that it was the will of Allah that a poor man should enter into Paradise 500 years before a rich man. This generosity attracted converts among the poor and later made it easier for Mohammed's followers to conquer countries where the poor lived in large numbers.

A succession of such raids on caravans was a help to the treasury of the new religious community, but it caused trouble between the warlike Moslems and the pacifist Jews. In the end, the Moslems drove some 700 Jews from Medina thus forcing them to abandon their possessions. These they used to provide housing and land for the 200 families who had migrated from Mecca in the Hegira. However, Mecca was waiting to avenge its earliest defeat, and a year later launched an attack on Medina with a force of about 3,000. Mohammed hastily gathered a force of more than 1,000 and met the invaders at Mount Uhud, six miles to the north of Medina. He was defeated and was carried from the battle unconscious and badly wounded. Though the Moslems were completely routed, the Meccans thought that they had taken enough revenge and did not press home their attack.

As soon as Mohammed had recovered from his wounds, he attacked a Jewish clan which he had accused of helping the Meccans. He took over their valuable date palm plantations for himself and his followers. In 626 the Koreish again attacked, and besieged Medina with an overwhelming force of 10,000 men. But, disheartened by chilly wind and rain, they raised the siege after 20 days. They did not attack the Moslems again.

In the next few years, Mohammed greatly extended his power by raiding the Jewish tribes, whom he now considered his enemies. At first, the Jews and the Moslems had gotten along well together. Both groups worshiped one God, whom the Jews had called Yahweh for thousands of years and whom the Moslems called Allah. Both revered Jerusalem as the Holy City. The Prophet hoped these similarities of belief would eventually lead the Jews to adopt his new religion and when this did not happen, he turned against them. In one instance, the Jewish tribe of Koraiza deserted from Mohammed's side during a battle with the Meccans. Having won the battle, Mohammed captured the warriors of the tribe and led them to the Medina market place, where he threatened to kill them all unless they would adopt Islam as their religion. Only one of the Jews agreed to do so and was spared. The rest, just about 800 in all, were butchered. In another case, Mohammed killed the chief of a Jewish tribe and took the chief's betrothed as his wife.

In 629, having made a truce with the Koreish, Mohammed led some 2,000 Moslems on a pilgrimage to Mecca. As his first service in the Medina mosque had established forever the simple ritual, so this first Moslem pilgrimage to the Kaaba established the ceremony that would be followed thereafter. The Meccans were so impressed by the discipline and fervor of the Moslems that several tribes outside the city offered their friendship to Mohammed.

Medina was now solidly behind the Prophet, but the loyalty of Mecca was divided. At first, Mohammed was not strong enough to take Mecca and had to sign a treaty with the ruling Koreish. After signing the truce, he began to strengthen his forces, and waited for

Islam was a fighting man's creed that promised the supreme reward for men who died in battle

an excuse to break the treaty. The excuse came when the Meccans attacked a tribe that was under Mohammed's protection. Mohammed marched on Mecca with an army of 10,000. When he entered the city, he was not opposed.

The unimportant Meccan trader had come a long way. He now lived with two wives and ten concubines as absolute ruler (under Allah) of much of Arabia. He lived simply in one or another of his wives' thatched huts. He drank no wine, lived frugally on dates and barley bread, mended his own clothes, swept out his room, and even milked the goats. His only surviving child was Fatima, whom his first wife Khadijah had borne him; he had no children by his other wives. Despite his simplicity he was vain, circling his much admired dark eyes with kohl, dying his hair, and using perfume freely. Though often silent and melancholy, he could become very sociable, mixing with rich and poor, and even with slaves, for whom he had a special liking because of the slave girl who had cared for him as a boy. And though he rebuked those who flattered him, he loved power.

Mohammed spent most of the last two years of his life in Medina, absorbed in the problems of administration and religion, and in further revelations, which he would announce in the mosque. He left no son to be his heir, but he left something more important, which was to expand over the centuries and was to rule from the borders of China to the Atlantic shores of Spain, from northern Africa to the Caucasus, in Egypt, Persia, northern India, and parts of Korea.

The Koran, even after some 13 centuries, is both scripture and law to all sects of Mohammedans. The series of revelations that came to the Prophet during his life applies to almost every part of the lives of the Faithful, from agriculture to daily washing and prayers, from the conduct of women and their place in Paradise to the administration of the mosque. The Koran is almost impossible to summarize, but its basic precepts are: prayer five times a day; the giving of alms to the poor; fasting once a year during the holy season of Ramadan; a pilgrimage to Mecca at least once in a lifetime. These are called the Four Duties necessary to salvation.

Islam was a poor man's religion, a fighting man's creed. That

Mohammed died in 632. Picture shows the Prophet's ascent to heaven

alone did much to account for the rapid growth of the Moslem empire. It was Islam, rather than the Arabs or Turks, that produced the Moslem conquests. Islam made life pleasant for the fighting man, for it gave him a belief in a supreme reward in Paradise if he died in battle. By promising special blessings to the poor, it encouraged oppressed races to submit to its code; it taught humanity toward women and children and even animals; and its emphasis on alms-giving led to one of the first welfare states the world has known. The Moslem conquest, by unifying many nations, assembled scholars of various races in schools and in libraries where they made discoveries in all the known sciences. Christian Europe was indebted to these Moslem scholars for many centuries thereafter.

Early Moslem empires have melted away, but the Moslems remain; and Islam remains a powerful force in many countries in North Africa and the Middle East as well as in such other countries as Indonesia, Malaysia and even Albania. Since the time of the original Moslem Empire, there have been other empires governed by Moslem conquerors. The Seljuk Turks, for example, ruled the Balkans until the early twentieth century. There have also been many attempts to rekindle the spirit of earlier times by uniting Moslems of all the Arab countries into one great Islamic nation. None of these attempts has been quite successful, but the dream of political unity among many Moslems remains a force in the politics of the Arab countries even today.

But whatever its political future, the Islamic religion unites 300,000,000 Moslems in a common faith and worship throughout the world. And the source of wisdom for all Moslems remains the same today as if it was for believers of the seventh century—Mohammed and his Koran.

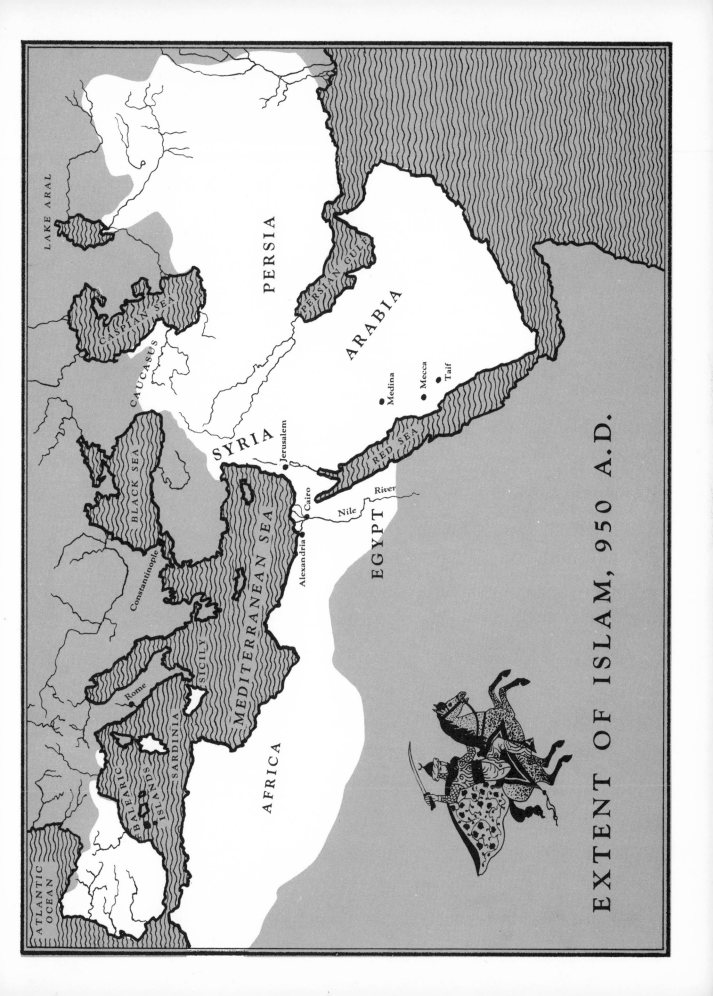

EXTENT OF ISLAM, 950 A.D.

LAKE ARAL

ATLANTIC OCEAN

CASPIAN SEA

CAUCASUS

BLACK SEA

Constantinople

Rome

MEDITERRANEAN SEA

SICILY

SARDINIA

BALEARIC ISLANDS

AFRICA

PERSIA

PERSIAN GULF

ARABIA

Medina

Mecca

Taif

SYRIA

Jerusalem

RED SEA

Cairo

Alexandria

Nile   River

EGYPT

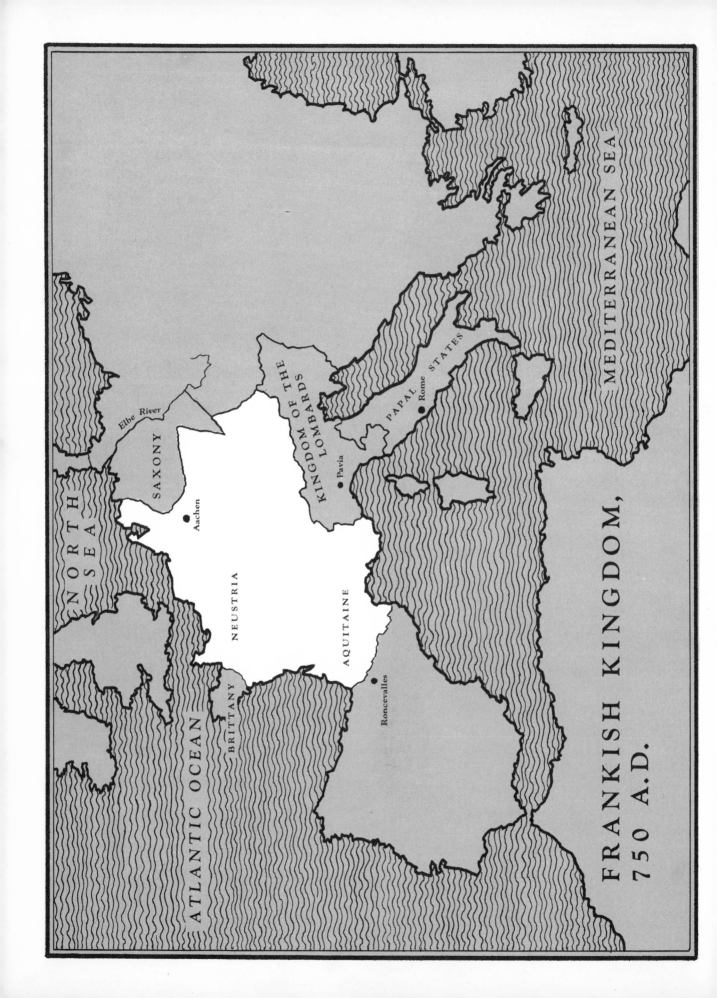

NORTH SEA

ATLANTIC OCEAN

MEDITERRANEAN SEA

SAXONY

Elbe River

Aachen

NEUSTRIA

BRITTANY

AQUITAINE

Roncevalles

KINGDOM OF THE LOMBARDS

Pavia

PAPAL STATES

Rome

FRANKISH KINGDOM, 750 A.D.

Charlemagne

Charles, the future Charlemagne, King of the Franks and Emperor of the Holy Roman Empire, was born April 2, 741, probably at Aachen, which in French is called Aix-la-Chapelle. He was the eldest son of Pepin III and grandson of Charles Martel (Charles of the Hammer), a great warrior whom Charles strongly resembled.

On Pepin's death Charles inherited half his father's kingdom of the Franks, the other half going to his younger brother Carloman. This made him ruler over Austrasia, Neustrasia and western Aquitaine. In 770 he married the daughter of Desiderius, King of the Lombards to the east, and so strengthened his influence in Italian politics. But after a year he repudiated his Italian princess and took to wife a Swabian lady, Hildegarde, who bore him three sons, Charles, Pepin, and Louis.

Desiderius not unnaturally took the return of his daughter as an insult, and began to ravage Lombardy in central Italy. Carloman had died in 771 and Charles was trying to subdue Saxony, a land to the east of his kingdom. Giving up that task, he turned to make war on his former father-in-law Desiderius. He met Desiderius with his army, beseiged Pavia, won the city, and was proclaimed King of the Lombards.

So his possessions grew. The Frankish kingdom earlier consisted of tiny dominions that had grown in the fifth century in what is now Belgium. As the kingdom spread outward, east, north and southwest, it eventually divided into two great powers, the French and the German. The people over whom Charles had become ruler were at various levels of civilization; their languages, racial types, customs, and religions in many cases differed widely from each other and from Charles's. The Saxons in the east were pagan, worshiping

Charlemagne, Charles the Great

with blood sacrifices the old Norse gods Odin and Thor. Charles was an ardent Christian and, throughout the years from 772 to 804, waged a total of 18 campaigns against the Saxons. Having conquered them at last, he gave them a choice: baptism or death. In one day he is said to have beheaded some 4,500 Saxons who refused Christianity.

By 805 he had subdued the Saxons on the northeast, driven back the advancing Slavs on the southeast, and won over Lombardy. He could now consolidate his gains and turn his attention to administration, which he loved even more than war.

His laws were such as would be made by any tough commander of an army of occupation. No Saxon assembly was lawful unless ordered by one of the Saxons whom Charles appointed as his Counts. The Christian clergy were to report to him on the work of the Counts, and were themselves protected by savage penalties against the still heathen Saxons. The Saxon law was modified to bring it closer to the customs of the Franks.

Such laws, along with Charles's wholesale butchery and deportation of Saxons, must be judged according to the period and to the problems Charles faced in trying to defend his developing empire. The Franks were not seamen and were at the mercy of increasing Viking raids from the north and Mohammedan raiders from the south. So it was vital for Charles to subdue the Saxon enemy in the east and, if possible, weld them into the small young empire to increase its strength.

The Franks were farmers and warriors. To create a middle class of traders and craftsmen, Charles protected the Jews. He allowed them to lend money at interest, a practice forbidden to Christians by the laws of the State and the Church.

In the ninth century, of course, printing had not yet been invented. All books were handwritten in Latin, which was the literary language of educated people in all European countries. Charles found, however, that many of the monks—the scholars of the day—could neither read nor write. He began to encourage education, and great men of learning began to flock to his capital at Aachen from all over Europe. Lectures and learned discussions were held there, and manuscripts were copied and revised. Today, museums have a few volumes dating back to that period. They are great treasures, with beautiful hand lettering and tiny decorative paintings around the initial letters and edges of the vellum pages. The bindings were often embossed with gold and studded with jewels. Books were precious and valued possessions.

Charles, who had great respect for learning, was himself one of the pupils, as were his wife Hildegarde, his sons, his daughters, and his secretary. He learned to read, though he never learned to write; he took it up too late in life, when he was too occupied to learn it well. But he loved to be read to as he sat at dinner. He brought to Aachen great priestly scholars, such as Alcuin from England, with whom he discussed astronomy, mathematics, rhetoric, and other learned subjects.

The reign of Charles saw the further establishment of the feudal system, originally brought about under Charles Martel. Feudalism had characteristics common to the Roman system wherein a landless nobleman or knight, who could not hope to protect himself, offered his services to a more powerful nobleman in return for support and protection. By making this agreement, the landless man became the "vassal" or servant of the nobleman who protected him. Developing as part of the system was the oath of fealty, or faithfulness, to the overlord, and the tradition of pride in a relationship by which, at its best, faith and service were due to both parties in the agreement—from vassal to lord and from lord to vassal. Charles Martel emphasized military service as an essential obligation of the system, according to which land was granted to the vassal, who, in return for his fief, or piece of land, furnished so many foot soldiers and so many horses.

For many centuries Europe was covered with a network of these fiefs. It was believed that the king, at the top, held his kingdom directly from God; his barons, in turn, held their lands from him, and so on down the scale to the serf, who worked the land of the freeman or nobleman. The system was a loose one, with countless variations

Decorated Frankish helmet is made of iron and bronze

Woodcut shows Charles giving instruction in palace school at Aachen

to fit local conditions, but almost all of today's more complicated civil services—judiciary, treasury, military—originally stem from the system which grew up during the ninth century.

Charles, restless without war and always busy, extended his lands to more than twice the size of the original Frankish kingdoms he had inherited from his father and brother. They now reached south to Rome, north along the borders of Dalmatia (a part of modern Yugoslavia), eastward through Bohemia (now Czechoslovakia) to the North Sea. On the southwest they included part of northern Spain from which, according to the legend, Charles had driven the Mohammedan invaders (or "Saracens") from Africa.

Despite the brutality of his wars, Charles was the most enlightened ruler Europe had seen for many centuries. He established a stable currency, kept waterways opened, and set regulations for weights, measures, and prices. He also controlled the use of forests and farmlands, protected trade, and encouraged architecture by building palaces and churches in many cities.

Charles used the priests, the only literate people of the day, as his civil servants. Out of this planned cooperation of Church and State emerged the Holy Roman Empire, which was to dominate Europe in centuries to come. Up to this time, the head of the Church in Rome had been subservient to the Emperor at Constantinople in what is now Turkey. Charles knew that a Roman Emperor in the West would greatly strengthen the Church in Rome. On November 24th, in the year 800, Charlemagne went to Rome with his court to celebrate the Nativity. On Christmas day, as Charles knelt before Pope Leo III to receive his blessing, the Pope produced a crown and set it upon the King's head, crowning him Emperor of the Holy Roman Empire. It was said that the King was not pleased, but he accepted the honor.

*Statuette of Charlemagne
from the Louvre Museum*

Pope Leo III crowns Charlemagne as Emperor of the Holy Roman Empire

From then on he felt it his duty to protect the Church and the Pope. But this complicated the struggle between church and state, which would last for centuries. The question would be whether a king was supreme in his own country and could do as he chose, or whether the Pope, as head of the Church of which the king and all his subjects were members, could dictate to him. The Pope had power to excommunicate a king and also to close all churches throughout the nation. This meant that for lack of confession and absolution, the whole population would go to purgatory when they died unless, of course, the king was powerful enough or skillful enough to get the ban lifted. The Pope could also declare a holy war, in which nations could earn favors in the hereafter by attacking the Pope's enemies. In the days when everyone believed in the Church's power, these were tremendous weapons.

Though on occasions of State, such as at his coronation, the Emperor put on all the elaborate embroidered regalia of the Roman Church—golden buckles, jeweled shoes, a gold crown set with precious gems—in ordinary life his garb was similar to that of his soldiers. This consisted of a linen shirt and breeches, covered by a fringed woolen tunic, banded hose, and leather shoes. In winter he would wear a long cloak of otter or martin skins. He always wore a

Charlemagne appears in robes of state,
bearing symbols of his power

Mounted on his horse, Charlemagne accepts the submission of an enemy

sword. The Emperor was very tall—6 feet 4 inches—with blond hair, lively blue eyes and a beak of a nose. He was stately and dignified. In the midst of battle his harsh, ringing voice could be heard shouting commands above the din.

Charles detested drunkenness and was a moderate eater. He loved hunting in the dense forests that covered Europe in those days, and often rode out with a great white hunting falcon on his wrist. He disliked banquets and preferred to dine to music, or be read to. Often, he would receive formal visits from his courtiers and subjects while he bathed and dressed.

Charles was very much a family man. He adored his daughters and could not bear to marry them off and see them leave home.

They, in turn, were devoted to him, and waited on him affection-
ately. They consoled themselves with lovers and bore illegitimate
children, whom Charles accepted into the household. He himself
kept a harem, in the half-Oriental fashion of his neighbors to the
east. Most women, it seems, preferred to share him than to have none
of him at all.

According to custom, and because of the danger of Viking raids
in southern France, Charles divided his empire among his three sons,
Pepin, Charles, and Louis. But Pepin died in 810, and Charles, the
second son, a year later. In 813, the Emperor proudly watched Louis,
the youngest of the three, crowned as the ruler of all his realm.

Many legends later grew up around Charlemagne, some of them
attributing to him the feats of his grandfather Charles Martel, or
even of Odin, greatest of the Saxon gods. One of the most famous
popular legends about Charles is preserved in the French *Song of*

The death of Charlemagne in 814. Legends say that he is only sleeping

Roland. This poem tells how Charles defeated the Saracens in battle at Roncesvalles in northern Spain and how he was tricked into withdrawing into France, leaving behind Roland in command. The Saracens attacked Roland, who fought until the last of his men had fallen, then blew on a great horn to summon Charles from across the Pyrenees. Charles returned with his army to find Roland dead and the Saracens in flight. Other legends said that Charles had not died, but was only sleeping and would waken at the hour of his country's greatest need. Charlemagne was made a Saint of the Church in 1165, and was even set among the stars. The Great Bear constellation is known in Germany as Karleswagen, and in England as Charles's Wain or Charles's Carriage.

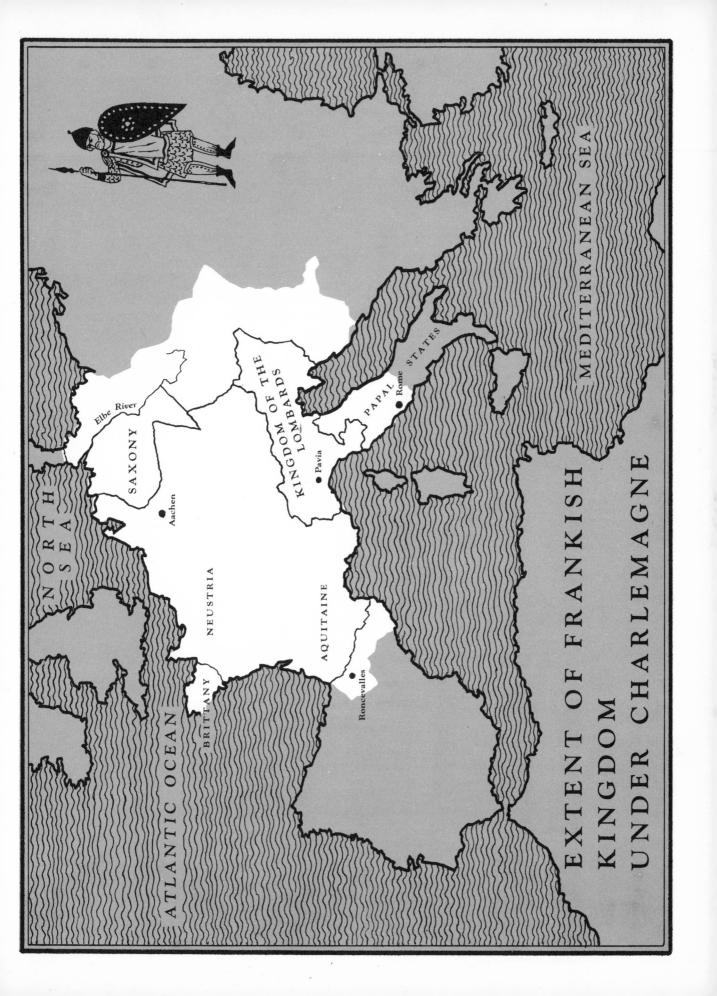

NORTH
SEA

Elbe River

SAXONY

Aachen

KINGDOM OF THE
LOMBARDS

Pavia

PAPAL
STATES

Rome

MEDITERRANEAN SEA

ATLANTIC OCEAN

BRITTANY

NEUSTRIA

AQUITAINE

Roncevalles

EXTENT OF FRANKISH
KINGDOM
UNDER CHARLEMAGNE

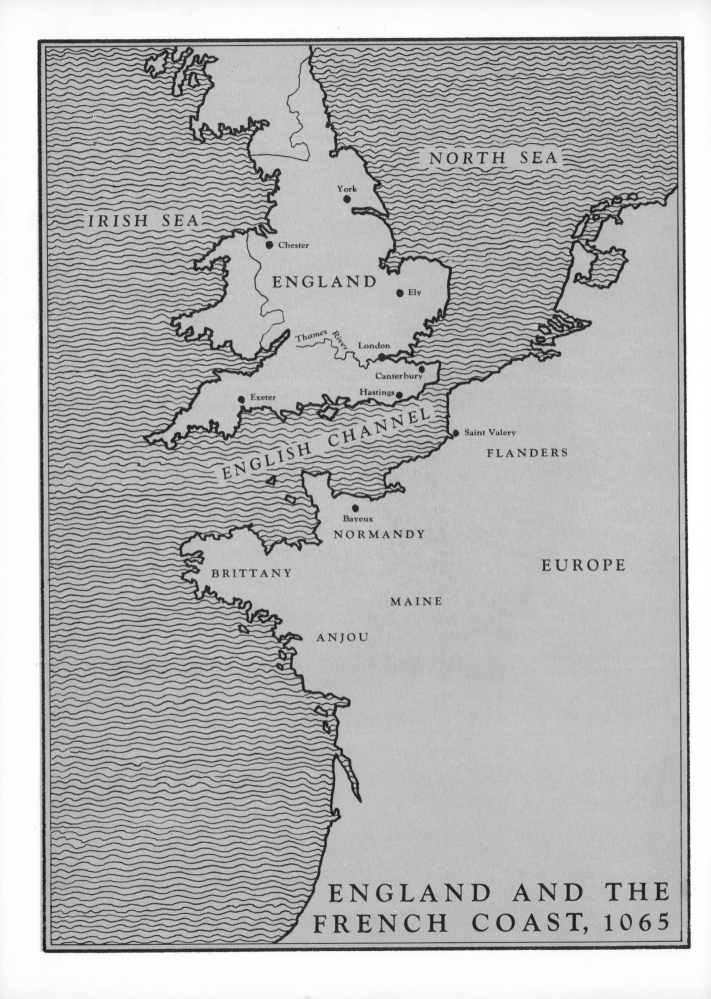

NORTH SEA

IRISH SEA

York

Chester

ENGLAND

Ely

Thames River
London

Canterbury

Hastings

Exeter

ENGLISH CHANNEL

Saint Valery

FLANDERS

Bayeux

NORMANDY

EUROPE

BRITTANY

MAINE

ANJOU

ENGLAND AND THE
FRENCH COAST, 1065

William the Conqueror

William, born in Normandy, was the son of Robert the Magnificent, the first Duke of Normandy, and his mistress Arlette, daughter of a master tanner. When the boy was four years old, Robert planned to go on a trip to the Holy Land. In case he might be killed on the way, he forced his barons to acknowledge William as heir to the dukedom. Robert died on the journey.

Young William's early years were difficult. The barons, hearing of Robert's death, broke their pledge and revolted. Three of the boy's guardians were murdered in turn, and for some years William was forced to hide among foresters and peasants in order to avoid a similar fate. It was probably at this time that he developed the cunning and ruthlessness of his later years.

When William claimed his right to the dukedom at 15, he asserted his leadership with considerable dignity and skill. He did not mind being illegitimate, and even at times signed himself Guilielmus Nothus (William the Bastard), but was ashamed of being descended from a common tanner. When he attacked the Norman town of Alençon, the garrison hung rawhides along the walls and beat on them with sticks as a taunt to the tanner's son. William stormed the gatehouse of the town, cut off the hands and feet of the guard and flung them over the walls into the town. The inhabitants then surrendered, and William dealt with them mercifully.

Except for the severity with which he punished opposition, he was a moderate and just ruler. He lessened the ill-treatment of peasants by their baron landlords and gave many rich gifts to the Church. He showed much patience and persistence in wooing Matilda, daughter of Baldwin, Count of Flanders, who at first declared that she would rather enter a nunnery than marry a bastard.

William I of England, Duke of Normandy

The marriage proved an unusually happy one for that rough age, and William was reputed to be consistently faithful to her.

It was by this marriage that William allied himself not, as would be expected, to neighboring Flanders but to Edward (the Confessor), King of England. For Matilda and Edward were both descended from Alfred the Great. In 1051, William, having signed a treaty with his neighbor on the east, Henry, King of the French, felt sufficiently secure against his neighboring dukes to pay a visit to Edward in England.

The old King, originally brought up in Normandy, was always homesick for that country and surrounded himself with Norman courtiers in his Saxon England. He took a liking to his brash young warrior kinsman. It was customary for a ruler to name his successor before he died, and as Edward had no sons, he promised the throne of England to William, Duke of Normandy.

The Duke returned home, fought and won several battles by which he annexed the region of Maine. Meanwhile, in England, Harold, Earl of Wessex and son of the powerful Earl Godwin who had long been adviser to King Edward, expected to be named king on Edward's death. Harold's brother Tostig had similar expectations.

In 1054 Harold was shipwrecked and captured on the shores of Normandy when on his way to visit King Henry. William held him prisoner; but the two men, somewhat alike in temperament, became fast friends, hunting together and going side by side in the fighting against Brittany. Harold even became betrothed to Agatha, one of William's daughters. But Harold was still a prisoner. When he wanted to return to England, William would let him go only on the condition that he swore to support the Duke's claim to the English throne. To make the oath more binding, William tricked him into making the promise over many hidden sacred relics.

In the dark hours of January, 1066, old Edward died and was buried before St. Peter's altar in the Westminster Cathedral he had built. Shortly thereafter the abbey walls resounded to the tread of Harold's men, whom he had summoned there to crown him king.

William immediately began to organize an invasion of England to claim the twice-promised throne. Through threats and offers of

Section of Bayeux Tapestry shows Harold swearing to support William

Huron School Library
Huron, Ohio

Tapestry shows part of the battle at Hastings where Harold was killed

rich plunder as reward he rounded up his nobles and their fighting men. The preparations took some months, for ships had to be equipped and provisioned—no small task. He insisted that the knights bring their own horses, which later proved to be one of the reasons for his success. Hitherto the Normans, like other Vikings, had invaded on foot and seized from the enemy what horses they needed. William, always strongly religious, also sought and gained the blessing of the Pope for his expedition.

There still exists an authentic pictorial record of the invasion of England. This is the Bayeux Tapestry, commissioned by Bishop Odo of Bayeux, William's half brother, for his new cathedral. It is a colorful strip of embroidery, 23 inches wide and 231 feet long. It depicts the building of the ships, the landing, the battle, and even the flight of Halley's Comet, which appeared in the sky and was thought a portent of great disaster by the superstitious of the day.

In the autumn of 1066 Harold received news that Harald Hardraada, King of Norway, had appeared on his northern coast with a fleet of dragon ships. He had come to support Tostig, Harold's brother, in his claim to the throne of England. Harold the Saxon made a hasty march north, defeated and killed Tostig and the King of Norway, and put the dragon ships to flight. Then, without rest, he had to bring his weary and wounded men back south to meet the Norman threat. Pausing only in London to add more fighting men, he turned southwest to oppose William's landing on the coast near Hastings.

The two armies faced each other on October 14th, 1066, on a hill later called Senlac, the Lake of Blood. They were nearly matched in numbers, approximately 7,000 to a side. They fought throughout the day, the mounted Normans charging against the archers and wall of shields of the stubborn Saxons. Toward nightfall Harold fell to a Norman arrow. Many of his leaders had already been killed, and at last the Saxons broke. The Norman victory was complete. Norman William had begun his conquest of Saxon England, and the history of Britain—perhaps of the world—was radically altered that day.

Such further resistance as the Saxons could patch together was ruthlessly crushed. By Christmas Day, William had seized London, and was able to have himself proclaimed King in Westminster Abbey, where even today, in a somewhat similar ceremony, all British monarchs are crowned. Early in the next year he made a formal tour through the southern counties, receiving submissions, disposing of the lands of those who had fought beside Harold, ordering the building of stone castles for his garrisons and the construction of new churches for his Norman clergy.

Now that Southern England had surrendered, William thought it safe to send for Matilda, who was in Normandy. She was crowned Queen in Westminster Abbey on Whitsunday two years after the invasion. Matilda was England's first actual queen, since the wives of earlier kings had not been crowned and had been called "Lady."

William's favoritism toward his Normans lost him the support of the old Saxon aristocracy. Rebellions broke out, and a considerable force gathered at York. William marched his army north to meet it. On the way he built stone castles in Warwick, Nottingham and finally in York itself. Each stronghold was commanded by

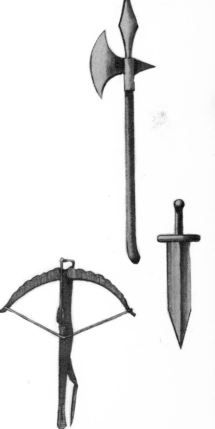

Norman weapons reflect the ferocity of 11th-century warfare

one of his men, and garrisoned. On the way back he built castles at Lincoln, Huntingdon, and Grimsby for his army of occupation.

Some of his leaders wanted to return to Normandy and their wives and lands for awhile. Since William had sent for Matilda to join him, he could hardly forbid his barons to visit their wives, but to prevent a mass exodus, which would weaken his forces to the point of danger, he decreed that any who went would lose the lands he had granted them in England.

This was wise, for in the following year another revolt broke out in Northumberland. William made a surprise march, slaughtered most of the rebels, ordered another castle to be built, and put one of his trusted barons in charge. The east of England had early been

Stone castle built by William as part of his kingdom in Normandy

Seal of William the Conqueror shows him as regent and warrior

settled by Danes, and when King Sweyn of Denmark appeared with his ships in the Humber in 1070, they rose. William marched north again, but King Sweyn retreated to his boats and did not offer battle. To punish the Danes of Yorkshire, William ordered the complete devastation of their land. Houses were burned, crops and livestock destroyed, and a famine followed such as England had not known since the days when these Danes had invaded the Saxon lands during the reign of King Alfred.

There was a short respite at Christmas time. Then William had to leave York and deal with trouble that had broken out at Chester in the west. Revolts spread like fires, so there was no time to lose; and William took the shortest route, over the Pennine hills in midwinter, through almost trackless forest and in snow so deep that his men had to march in single file, leading their horses. They grumbled and tried to mutiny, but there was no way but forward.

The remarkable march took the rebels by surprise, and William was again victorious. William paid off his mercenaries, rewarding the loyal ones but retaining those who had threatened to desert for a longer term of service. Since Chester was an important post controlling the unruly Welsh border, William ordered another castle built and left behind a commander and a garrison.

Now that there was peace in the kingdom William turned his energies to administration. He did not attempt to enforce Norman law upon the newly conquered Saxons, but allowed them to follow their old customs. He was comparatively humane, for his period. In his reign no man was hanged, even for murder, though blinding and mutilation—the common punishments of the age—were inflicted.

William spent Easter of 1070 in Winchester. Since this was the ancient capital of the Saxons he had himself crowned again, this time by three Cardinals sent over by the Pope for this special purpose. The Cardinals also served William by deposing, on orders from the Pope, the Saxon Stigand, Bishop of Winchester and Archbishop of Canterbury. Stigand soon died in prison in Winchester. In his place William, with the approval of the Pope, appointed his old Norman friend Lanfranc. In a day when the authority of the Church was second only to the power of the King, this was an important move.

After a short period of tranquillity another Danish invasion threatened, this time around the Isle of Ely. William had made a truce with the Danish fleet wintering in the Humber, but his scorched-earth policy ashore had left them hungry. King Sweyn of Denmark now returned to them with reinforcements, and they moved further south to the fens and the Isle of Ely.

Among the rebellious English who joined them was a thane, a knight of Lincolnshire, Hereward the Wake. This strong and able leader knew all the hidden ways through the fens and marshes that surrounded the high mound of Ely with its Benedictine monastery and cathedral. Hereward constantly harried the Normans who tried to lay siege to the place, and his success attracted more and more Saxon knights.

William bought off King Sweyn and his fleet, and this left Hereward without support from the sea. The island was well defended and the Norman cavalry could not operate through the marshes, but the Benedictine monks turned traitor in exchange for William's promise to spare them and their rich lands. Hereward succeeded in escaping through the marshes to a boat, but most of his followers were slaughtered by the Normans. Some years later Hereward made peace with William and actually fought on his side in Normandy.

The crushing of this second Danish revolt completed the ruthless subjugation of the countryside. There were no further risings, and William could turn his attention to the problems of government. The Norman conqueror of England ruled with a firm hand. Like his Viking ancestors, statesmen, warriors, or pirates, he believed all weakness harmful, all strength good. In a sense he was right, for the result was a stable England, its varied people combined under one rule.

From the Welsh border at Chester, east to Newcastle-upon-Tyne; south through York, Lincoln and London to Canterbury; west through Exeter to Tintagel, William bestowed Saxon lands on Norman earls, and ordered that the wooden castles be rebuilt in stone. So William brought Norman architecture to England, along with Norman methods of administration that he had used in his own dukedom. To collect information about his new kingdom he ordered a list to be made of all the fiefs he had granted, and of all the people and their possessions in these fiefs. This survey of national resources was known as the Domesday, or Doomsday, Book. It was so called because, like the religious Day of Judgement—or Day of Doom—there was no appeal from it. It became an invaluable basis for taxation and administration.

The Normans were few and the Saxons many. To suppress a strong but unorganized resistance movement, William, like many other commanders of an army of occupation since his day, imposed a curfew. Curfew meant "cover-fire," and when the sundown bells rang in a town all men had to be indoors and to cover their fires for the night. In a country where the thatched-roof wooden houses had no chimneys this was a useful precaution against fire. It also meant that small benighted groups of Norman travelers would not be cut up under cover of darkness.

William's laws were reasonably just for the times, and a number of Saxon landowners who had been dispossessed vowed loyalty to the new King and were allowed to buy back their lands and castles. He had been harshly criticized for destroying some 40 "towns"

Section of the Domesday Book, a record of resources in William's English realm to create a royal hunting preserve still called the "New Forest," but the towns were only small villages. And his action had a practical purpose. Hunting on horseback with spear and bow was an important means of keeping mounted knights in condition for warfare, so the royal preserves functioned as training grounds.

Though he was so occupied in England, William kept close control over Normandy, to which Matilda had returned shortly after her coronation. He considered England a possession of Normandy, and it was only later that the English kings thought of Normandy as an English possession. It was not until the reign of Mary Tudor that Calais, the last vestige of Normandy ruled by England, reverted to France.

Now that England was pacified, Normandy began to give trouble. And the main cause was William's eldest son Robert. Just as William's father had named him as successor before going on a crusade, so William in turn named Robert as the future Duke of Normandy. When William became king of England, Robert demanded that he should become Duke of Normandy. William refused, on the grounds that he was still alive, remarking "It is not my custom to remove my clothes until I go to bed."

Robert was not easily discouraged. Nicknamed "Curthose" by his father because of his short legs, the boy was powerfully built, an expert with sword and crossbow, eloquent, charming, and extravagant. He was popular, ambitious, surrounded by young and flattering friends, and his mother's favorite.

When further friction developed between William and Robert, the two younger sons, Richard and William, took their father's side, but Matilda stood by her favorite. Bad feeling increased to the point where Robert fled from Normandy and begged help in money and men from the French barons, who were on bad terms with the Normans. From time to time, during William's absence in England, Matilda sent Robert gold and silver from the ducal treasury. William reproached Matilda for giving aid to his enemies, and this led to a bitter quarrel between them.

After three years Robert had collected enough of his father's enemies, including his cousin King Philip of France, to start open

French statue shows William gallantly leading his men into battle

hostilities. From the castle of Gerberoy, lent to him by Philip, he sent raiding parties over the border into Normandy.

William was spending Christmas at Rouen when news came to him of his son's open rebellion. He collected all the barons who, with their men, were attending the Feast of the Nativity, and in midwinter marched on Gerberoy. His English and Norman soldiers laid siege to the French and Normans in the castle, but without much success. One tradition records that father and son came face to face in battle and that Robert, after unseating his father from the saddle, dismounted and helped him to remount. The castle finally fell to William, but only after he had persuaded King Philip to withdraw his support from Robert. In the view of the Norman barons this was so close to failure that they began to lose confidence in William and to shift their allegiance to Robert.

Robert was pardoned, and to place him out of mischief was sent to hold the northern English frontier against Malcolm of Scotland. But Robert's extravagance and his arrogant refusal to obey orders brought on a final quarrel. William banished Robert from his court, and the two never again met.

Misfortunes began to come thick and fast. William's beloved Matilda, who had quarreled with him over Robert, died in Caen in November, 1083, still unreconciled. Richard, the third son and too young to be knighted, died from a fall from his horse when hunting in the New Forest. Naturally, William's enemies claimed that this was a divine punishment for evicting the inhabitants of the area to make the forest.

Agatha, William's daughter who had given her heart to the handsome young Saxon Harold, was now ordered to marry the King of Galicia, an old friend who had fought beside William at the Battle of Hastings where Harold had been killed. She set off for Spain with a large escort of priests and nobles but, perhaps grieving for Harold, died on board ship. Her body was brought back for burial in Bayeux cathedral. Cicely, another daughter, died as Abbess of the convent in Caen in which Matilda had been buried.

During his remaining years William conquered but did not entirely pacify much of Scotland and Wales. His main achievement

Bayeux Tapestry, ordered by Bishop Odo, records the Norman invasion

was in administration. To stimulate trade and craftsmanship, which the feudal system did little to encourage except in the arts of building and weaponry, he brought in and protected the Jews. As money-lenders they were to become essential to the early growth of urban communities as distinct from those based on land-holding. He granted a charter to London, allowing the city to elect its own officials and to a large extent administer its own laws. As trade increased in subsequent reigns other towns obtained royal charters on the same model. This practical form of government did much to save England from some of the more rigid ways of continental feudalism. But perhaps the greatest boon that William conferred on unwilling England was the firm government that allowed the gradual evolution of Celt, Saxon, Dane and Norman into the nation called English.

The Bayeux Tapestry gives some 17 pictures of William the Conqueror, on foot, on horseback, at table, and on his throne. He is shown as a very tall man, dark haired, with the massive shoulders of his warrior breed, smooth-faced, with hair shaved at the back. But as he grew older and embittered he found solace in eating. In fact he became so fat that he had difficulty in mounting his horse. Even this did not prevent his going to war. But in Normandy he quarreled with King Philip of France, captured Nantes, and sacked and burned the city.

It was his last of many victories. As he rode in triumph through the still smouldering ruin his horse stumbled on a hot ember. William was thrown heavily against the iron pommel of his saddle. Carried in great pain to the town of Caen, he died there from his injury. By chance, but perhaps as his final wish, he was buried there, reunited at last with Matilda.

The Norman adventurer had built a solid administration in conquered England. It survived 14 years of rule by his second son, the detested William II (Rufus). Like his brother Richard, he also died in the New Forest, but by assassination. The fourth son, Henry, named Beauclerc (the Handsome Scholar), then took the throne.

IRISH SEA

NORTH SEA

York

Chester

ENGLAND

Ely

Thames River

London

Canterbury

Hastings

Exeter

ENGLISH CHANNEL

Saint Valery

FLANDERS

Bayeux

NORMANDY

EUROPE

BRITTANY

MAINE

ANJOU

ENGLAND AND THE
FRENCH COAST, 1087

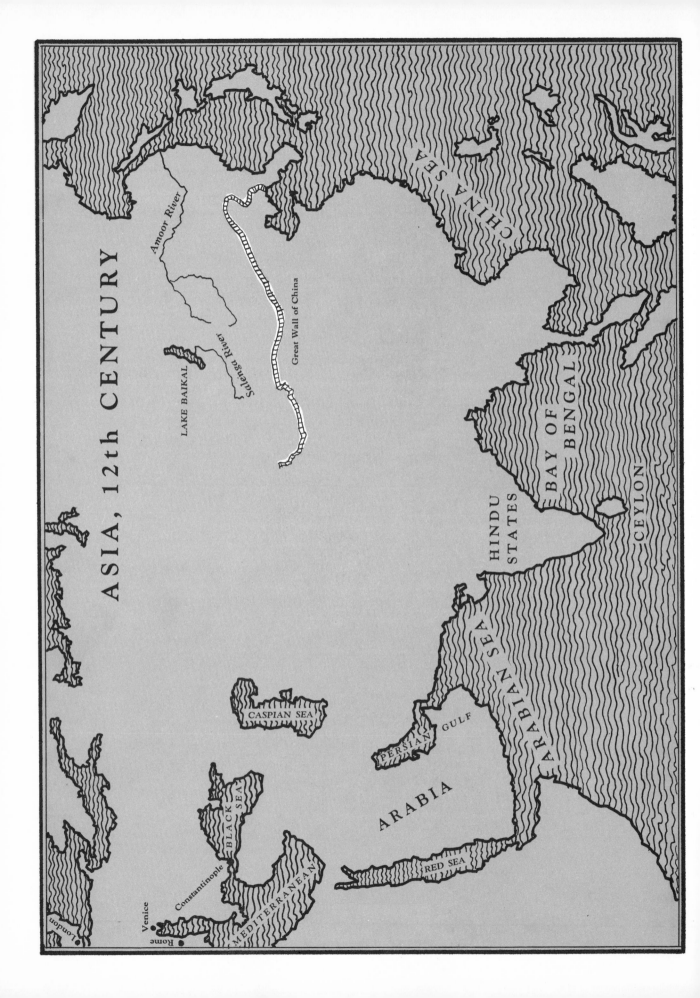

Genghis Khan

In the twelfth century a group of nomadic Mongol tribesmen grazed their vast herds of sheep and rough-coated ponies north of the border of China, as they had done for centuries. They lived in flimsy, felt-covered huts and tents, moving north with the herds in summer and south in the winter. They raced horses, ate horse meat, drank mare's milk, and hunted on horseback. Using their horses both as means of transport and as their chief source of food, they engaged in incessant intertribal warfare.

Barring their way to the south lay the Great Wall of China and the Kin Empire. South of the Kin Empire lay its rival, the Sung Empire, which ruled the rest of China. Cut off from the fertile southlands by these two great empires, hemmed in to the north, east, and west by land even more bleak than their own rolling steppes, the Mongols seemed unlikely to create history.

Such was the situation when in 1162, a Mongol chief named Yesukai returned home from a successful foray in which he had defeated a rival named Temujin. As he dismounted before the felt tent of one of his wives, he learned that she had just borne him another son. The camp buzzed with excitement, for the baby had been delivered firmly grasping in his right hand a small blood clot, like a red pebble.

To the Mongols, this foretold that the child would grow up to be a conqueror, a shedder of blood. For some reason, Yesukai chose to name his new son after Temujin, the man he had just conquered.

When Yesukai died, Temujin was only 13 years of age. For lack of a strong leader, the tribe, said to number about 40,000 huts, began to drift apart. But Temujin's mother, by persuasion and by force, managed to preserve half of her husband's fighting force until

Genghis Khan,
The Perfect Warrior

her son came of age. With this nucleus Temujin fought his way up until he controlled larger and larger groups of the Mongol tribes.

It took him thirty years to unite the tribes under his command. During this time of tough cavalry warfare and cunning diplomacy, Temujin learned tactics and strategic planning and forged an army. His principle of discipline was simple and effective—the penalty for disobedience was death.

In the year 1206, at the age of 44, Temujin decided that the time had come to consolidate his position. He called together his lesser chieftains on the banks of the Onon River in Siberia and proclaimed himself Genghis Khan (Very Mighty King, or The Perfect Warrior).

Though in his middle years, Genghis was still hardy from life in the saddle and from sleeping in felt tents and in the open air. His normal diet had been horse meat, mare's milk, and cheese, but like his followers he did not mind eating cats, fierce watchdogs, rats and lice, or drinking blood—hardly human fare. He was short and stocky, with the typical slanted eyes and round head of the Mongols, and so tough that he ignored cold and fatigue. He was expert in the use of sword, dagger, spear, and bow. Wives were a sign of power among the Mongols, and Genghis is said to have had 500 of them.

The first step in establishing his position as leader was to defeat and slay in battle his only remaining rivals within the tribe. This freed him from danger at home and allowed him to turn his attention to the Kin Empire, which ruled the south of China. Genghis's intelligence service was excellent, for many of his followers had served as mounted troops under the Kin rulers.

He was familiar enough with the Chinese people to know that the peasants would not fight for the Kin emperors. Furthermore he hoped that the Khitan nobles, who had only recently been conquered by the Kin, would come over to his side. Genghis felt that the Chinese warriors had grown soft behind their city walls and would offer no strong opposition to his fierce Mongols. The Khitan Tartars from Manchuria had successfully attacked the Kin Empire, as had the Golden Tartars. It was now time for Genghis and his Mongolian Tartars to have their turn.

Genghis began by capturing Hia, the crossroads city where the routes to Burma and Tibet met. Then he retired to reassemble his army. On the western side of the Great Wall, he met and defeated an army led by the son of the Kin Emperor and led his own army through the wall. Then, parcelling out his command among his sons and brothers, he launched a three-pronged attack. The south wing was commanded by his three sons; the southeast was under his own command; in the east, near the sea, was his left wing, commanded by three of his brothers.

Town after town fell before his swift, disciplined, and seasoned horsemen. The success of the Mongols led many Kin commanders to desert to Genghis with their men. The Sung Empire to the south also assisted him against the Kin. Pekin (now Peking), the Kin capital was captured, the country was overrun as far as the Hwangho River, and the great Kin Empire was reduced to a small triangle beside the sea in the southeast.

Apparently Genghis intended from the first that this should be

Temujin summoned his chieftains and named himself **Genghis Khan**

no mere foray, but conquest and occupation. He was now undisputed lord of a vast, wealthy territory, whose craftsmen could produce an unlimited number of weapons, including gunpowder and crude firearms. Genghis secured the services of an able Chinese assistant, who helped him to establish an administration that went far beyond the mere collection of taxes. It undertook the building and maintenance of roads and performed other public services. But, perhaps fearful of growing weak from too many civilized comforts, the conqueror continued to live among the tents of Karakoram.

Meanwhile another Mongol chieftain had, by treachery, penetrated among the Mohammedan Turki people around Samarkand and established himself as King there between China and Kharismian. Genghis lost no time in conquering the territory and eliminating this new threat. His boundaries now adjoined those of Kharismia. He sent an offer of peace and trade to the Shah of Kharismia, and the offer was accepted. Now, secure in his rule of the East, Genghis began to think of moving west.

Far off to the southwest, another nomadic people, the Arabs, had extended their rule from Baghdad to Egypt and Palestine. Spurred by a strong Islamic zeal, a Turki people had built up a small but rich empire on the famous east-west trade route around Samarkand. In the same period, Europe had added to her other troubles a series of disorganized, corrupt, and ineffective crusades to regain Jerusalem from the Moslem Arabs. The Mongol Khan dreamed of conquering these lands to the west, but no one in the Western world was in a position to worry about the aggressive aims of an obscure Tartar horde almost a world away.

War chariots were used against the Mongols by the Chinese

A Mongol youth, mounted on horseback, salutes the great Genghis Khan

The Mongol invasion of the West began almost by chance. Genghis had signed a treaty with the Shah of Kharismia, but soon after this a party of Mongol traders were put to death by the governor of Ortrar, who was a subordinate of the Shah. Genghis demanded the surrender of the governor, and the Shah responded by beheading the leader of the Mongol delegation that brought him Genghis's message. If it had not been for this insult, Genghis Khan might have remained an obscure Mongol chieftain, with barely a mention in the history books of Europe. Because of it, the Mongol hordes were to

Painting shows armed Mongol warrior tightening the cinch on his saddle

sweep across to the very frontiers of Europe, whole civilizations were to be erased, and many millions were to die.

Genghis declared war on the Shah. The Khan's army, perfected in discipline and mobility, skilled in the use of siege weapons and led by expert strategists, now acquired a new weapon—extreme and calculated cruelty. In the first battle, the Shah's army of 400,000 is said to have left 160,000 dead on the field. Otrar was sacked; Bokhara was burned. Samarkand and the other cities surrendered, but were not spared. Merv, with its famous libraries, was among the cities that surrendered; in 13 days over 1,000,000 men, women, and children in the city were butchered. Mishapur, Ravy, and Herat suffered the same fate.

Along with cruelty, Genghis used treachery of every kind as a means of warfare. Captives were marched in front of the Mongol armies as human shields. When a city fell, the inhabitants were raped and slaughtered. The aim was total devastation and total depopulation. This kind of warfare set the pattern for all future Mongol advances. The Mongols engulfed Russia and extended their control from Korea in the north to Delhi in the south. They reached the Caspian Sea and the Dnieper River and inspired terror as far off as Constantinople. They established an empire in northern China that was to endure until 1356.

In 1227, when his troops were defeating the Russians north of the Caspian Sea, Genghis was directing a campaign in western China. Astrological signs persuaded him that he was about to die. Hastening homeward, he was taken ill in what is now Kansu Province in northwest China. He pressed on to reach his traveling lodge on the fringes of Mongolia, and died there in his sixty-fifth year.

He had named his son, Ogotai, as his successor. But if the Khan's death were to be made public before Ogotai was actually proclaimed Khan in his place, many rivals might appear. The funeral cortege proceeded northward in secret to the river Kerulen, where the body of Genghis Khan was taken round in turn to the encamp-

Genghis Khan receives a "shongar" or falcon offered to him in tribute

ments of his more important wives. The escort killed every peasant and traveller they encountered, so that no one would spread the word of the conqueror's death.

Other Mongol invasions followed those of Genghis Khan, though few were as devastating. The Mongols were fearless warriors, but had little ability in government or in winning the allegiance of conquered peoples. Within a few centuries they had been absorbed by the Russians, the Chinese, and the Turks. They left no legacy of literature, art, or architecture for the world to remember them by. Instead, they are remembered as masters of a policy of total warfare, scorched earth, and unlimited cruelty.

MONGOL EMPIRE, 13th AND 14th CENTURIES

CHINA SEA

Amoor River

LAKE BAIKAL

Salenga River

Great Wall of China

BAY OF BENGAL

HINDU STATES

CEYLON

ARABIAN SEA

CASPIAN SEA

PERSIAN GULF

ARABIA

BLACK SEA

Constantinople

RED SEA

MEDITERRANEAN

Venice

Rome

London

Frederick II

Frederick II was the grandson of Frederick Barbarossa (Red Beard), the Holy Roman Emperor. He was the son of Henry VI and Constance of Naples. Constance was 42 years old when she bore him. It was most important that the birth of so important a royal offspring should not be suspected of fraud. So she commanded that a tent be erected in the marketplace of Jesi, near Ancona, Italy, and the birth of her son occurred there, in sight of all.

Frederick's ancestors were the Norman kings of Sicily and the great Hohenstaufen princes of Germany. At the age of two he was elected by the barons and princes to be King of Germany. Following the death of his father one year later, the small boy succeeded Henry as King of Sicily. Constance acted as regent until her death shortly thereafter.

Constance had appointed Pope Innocent III as Frederick's guardian and regent. The Pope accepted the trust only on condition that Sicily and Germany, ruled by Henry as one kingdom, should be divided. He felt that so strong an alliance was a threat to his own power. Beyond this pledge Innocent paid scant attention to the boy. The selection of a tutor, Honorius, later to become Pope, proved of considerable importance. Though the young King was often neglected and even hungry, he had an excellent education.

The mixed population of Palermo, where he grew up, gave him fluency in six languages, including Arabic. His knowledge of Arabic language and culture was to prove invaluable, for it enabled him to see Christianity from the Islamic viewpoint of the Sicilian Saracens.

At the age of 12 years, Frederick became impatient of the guardianship and dismissed his teachers. At 14 he was legally of age, and a year later he married Constance of Aragon. Then he set out to

Frederick II, Holy Roman Emperor, King of Sicily and of Jerusalem

reclaim the crown of Germany which the Pope had forced him to relinquish to Otto IV. He had his baby son crowned King of Sicily, to hold the throne in his absence. Now in 1211, Otto was deposed by the princes of Germany, and Frederick was invited to accept the throne, this time with the support of the Pope. The chance was too good to miss. To gain even further support, Frederick made an alliance with Philip II of France.

In 1213, at Eger in the northwest corner of Bohemia, Frederick made a further agreement with the Pope. Under oath he promised not to combine his two crowns by resuming the rule of Sicily that he had passed on to his son. He was to support the Pope, to place the German Church under the Pope's sole authority and to aid the Roman Church in suppressing heresy. Later this oath was to cause Frederick much trouble. Its immediate result was that, with the powerful aid of Philip II of France, he routed Otto at the battle of Bouvines in 1214 and made good his claim to the throne.

At the age of 20, young Frederick was probably quite sincere in accepting the Pope's terms, and they were laid down in what is called the Golden Bull of Eger (a bull is a papal document named after the lead seal—in Latin, a *bulla*—attached to it). He had been tutored by clergy, and his royal ministers were also priests, since learning was almost the monopoly of the Church. As the young King of Sicily, ruling over an island split among the quarrelsome German barons, he had been little more than a figurehead. To maintain his authority over these barons, each with his own castle and court of justice, he had needed the moral support of the Pope.

The Italy of the Middle Ages was divided into many territories, each governed from its most important city—such as Venice, Naples, Milan, Florence, Parma. The greatest of these city-states was the Papal State which was, of course, ruled from Rome. Germany was also split among several principalities, many of them ruled by bishops. But the Roman Church owned more land than any noble or minor king, though its territory was scattered around Europe and its Papal States in Italy were comparatively small and defenseless.

Frederick, as a loyal servant of the Pope, King of Germany, and ruler of the Holy Roman Empire, could be of great value to the security of the Papal States. But a Frederick grown so powerful might also be a threat to the Pope in Sicily and southern Italy, endangering papal supremacy in the south. This is why the Pope demanded that he give up Sicily. And as a condition for the support of the King of France, it seemed prudent to bind him by other vows. One of these was that he take part in a crusade against the Saracens in Palestine.

Even before the battle of Bouvines, Pope Innocent III had tied up his protégé in every way possible. But two years later he died, and Frederick's one-time tutor became Pope Honorius III. It seems probable that Frederick and Honorius were personal friends, so far as their official positions permitted. There was a notable change in the relations between Frederick and the Papacy. In 1220 Frederick's son Henry, already King of Sicily and Frederick's heir to the German Holy Roman Empire, was elected by the Germans "King of the Romans" with no protest from the Pope. Honorius allowed Frederick to rule Sicily during his lifetime, thus freeing him from the first condition of the Golden Bull. It may have been in return for this that Frederick confirmed his crusading oath, made seven years before, and granted rights and liberties to the landowning dignitaries of the Church in Germany, making them independent barons, or even princes.

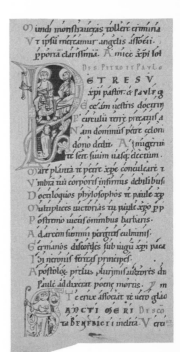

Frederick, still only in his twenties, was remarkably mature in planning his policies. He might easily have spent his energies on his northern kingdom, but he much preferred the pleasant life and warm sun of Sicily and southern Italy. So he sent his son Conrad IV to Germany and himself remained in Sicily to secure his base of operations. But, despite the agreeable climate, he did not waste his time. Between 1221 and 1225 he subdued the Sicilian barons and brought the whole island into a single unit, establishing royal government, a single system of laws, and a judicial system. He also established markets and fixed just prices for goods. Since metal was scarce at the time, he issued leather tokens in place of coins. From this practice developed the modern use of paper money in place of gold and silver.

Much of Frederick's time was spent in reading; he commissioned handwritten manuscripts such as this

Now that Sicily and his court at Palermo were reasonably safe, Frederick realized that his ambitions would shortly bring him into conflict with the Papacy. The Papacy had two weapons. It could ex-communicate him; this would mean closing the church doors to all his subjects, thus forbidding marriages, baptism, and the forgiveness of sins. Or it could preach a crusade against him. Either of these actions would free his Christian subjects from their loyalty to the king, and make them unwilling to fight for him.

Frederick found an answer. That was to use Moslem Saracens, over whom he had established control, as his first defense. The thunderings from Rome would mean nothing to them. On his northern border Frederick established two big garrison colonies of warrior Saracens, one at Lucera near the spur of Italy, the other at Nocera, near Naples. There was another hole he must plug in his defences. His advisers and ministers were all churchmen, but they owed obedience to their bishops and the Pope as much as to their king. This

Hunting with his trained falcons was one of Frederick's favorite sports

Official seal of Frederick II

could be dangerous. To create a supply of future civil servants independent of religious orders, Frederick founded, in 1224, the University of Naples and a medical school at nearby Salerno.

A year later he married Yolande de Brienne, and through her became King of Jerusalem. This was in name only, since Palestine was in the hands of the Saracens of the Islamic Empire. But some day the title might be of use.

In 1226 the Golden Bull of Rimini established the fighting order of the Teutonic Knights, theoretically under the Pope. But it was Frederick who organized them in his German Kingdom, endowed the order, and honored it. Within three years the Teutonic Knights were to prove their value.

His preparations completed, Frederick, now 32 years of age, was ready to expand his kingdoms. He laid claim to Lombardy, the area in northern Italy between the Po River and the Alps. Lombardy and the city-states of central Italy and the Rhineland were alarmed and formed leagues for self-defense. Honorius, the friend of Frederick, had died, and had been succeeded by Pope Gregory IX, who decided to stop Frederick's move. He ordered Frederick to make good his vow at Eger and start on a crusade against the Saracens of the Holy Land.

Frederick was no fanatic Christian. In fact, it was beginning to be said that he was a Mohammedan, for his court was Oriental in its luxury, with Saracen guards, and eunuchs to tend the women of the harem. His own interests were without bounds. He entertained poets, philosophers, and learned Jews and Moslems as guests. Mathematics, astrology, philosophy, alchemy, all interested him. He kept a zoo, but for study, not for amusement; he wrote a book on hawking and birds in general; he fostered algebra and Arabic numerals in Europe. Hunting was his favorite amusement, but he loved witty conversation. He wrote brilliantly in Latin, Greek, and Arabic.

At this time, however, Frederick did not dare challenge Pope Gregory. He collected a fleet, and was ready to embark with 40,000 troops. But plague broke out among the men, and they deserted in great numbers. Frederick himself caught it and was unable to maintain personal control over his army.

Pope Gregory did not care if the King died, sword in hand, in Palestine, or of the fever. He wanted the King out of Italy at any cost. So he put Frederick under the ban of excommunication. Frederick replied with pamphlets attacking the corruption of the Church. These were so effective in stirring up the citizens of Rome that Pope Gregory had to flee the city. It was Frederick who calmed the Romans, thus allowing Gregory to return. It is no wonder that Frederick won the nickname *Stupor mundi et immutator mirabilis*— "Wonder of the world and marvelous innovator."

In seven months Frederick had recovered from the plague and this time set forth on the crusade. As soon as he was safely at sea the vindictive Gregory renewed the excommunication, absolved his subjects from loyalty to their King, sent out monks to spread a rumor of Frederick's death, and proclaimed a crusade against the absent crusader. Soon the Pope's army had conquered most of southern Italy and Sicily. Not content with this, Gregory sent two delegates to Acre, in Palestine, forbidding Frederick's crusaders to obey his commands. Gregory thus hindered, by his own desire for power, the very crusade he had ordered.

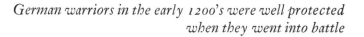

German warriors in the early 1200's were well protected when they went into battle

The attitude of Malik al Kamil, the Saracen commander in Palestine, was a pleasant contrast to the hostility of the head of the Christian Church. The Saracen was delighted to find in Frederick a Christian who spoke fluent and even witty Arabic, and knew Moslem ways and literature. He made a personal treaty with the King, granting him Nazareth, Bethlehem, and Jerusalem, and allowing him free passage between Jerusalem and the coast for a period of ten years.

Visored basinett or helmet like those worn by Frederick's soldiers

Frederick entered the Holy City of Jerusalem almost alone, and peacefully. His aim was to be crowned in the Church of the Holy Sepulchre. But as no clergy could officiate under Gregory's ban he placed the crown on his own head. Some Knights of the religious order of Templars tried to betray him to Malik al Kamil for assassination, but the amused Malik sent the letter on to Frederick. When he boarded his ship at Acre, Christian bystanders pelted him with filth and foul abuse.

The crusades were a strange series of adventures, and this, the Sixth Crusade, had been the oddest of them all. Gregory's attempt to rid Italy of his enemy had failed. Frederick, excommunicated, deprived of authority over his own Christian troops, plotted against and abused by the local Christians, had secured for them the holy places of their religion, and safe passage for all Christian pilgrims up to the year 1244. Jerusalem was not to be in Christian hands again until 1918.

The Teutonic Knights, created in the previous century, had remained loyal to Frederick, even though when he landed back in Brindisi almost all his kingdom of Sicily seemed lost to him. But his people received him joyously. A brisk campaign freed Sicily of the Pope's army, and a threat to invade the papal lands forced Gregory to remove the excommunication and make peace. To save the Pope's pride, Frederick promised Gregory to protect papal lands and to acknowledge that the Pope was, officially, overlord of Sicily. But, like Gregory, the Emperor was prepared to renew the struggle for power later on.

Now the Holy Roman Empire, i.e., Germany, needed immediate attention. Henry, who had come of age in 1228 while Frederick was on crusade, reversed his father's wise policy of creating principalities, and favored the growth of city-states. Frederick in 1231 reversed this policy again, and Henry revolted. But he submitted to his father and was pardoned. In that same year Frederick completed his reorganization of Sicily. Private armies among the barons, private wars, and private courts of law were abolished. In the future, supreme power was to be vested in the King. Clergy and religious institutions were no longer exempt from taxes. And it seems that the new University of Naples, founded by Frederick, had produced its expected crop of literate laymen for the civil service, because men in religious orders were now barred from public office. Though the Pope was still nominally overlord of Sicily, his clergy could no longer influence policy.

In 1235, when Frederick was again called back to Germany by the second revolt of his son Henry, he deposed and imprisoned his son and brought him back to Sicily. While in Germany, Frederick modernized and attempted to centralize the administration, as he had done in Sicily.

From Italy the Emperor sent back another son, Conrad, to be King of the Romans and go forth to smash the Lombard League of the cities of northern Italy. Gregory now saw himself threatened from Lombardy in the north, and by the Sicilian Kingdom in the south. He was further affronted by Frederick's reorganization of the administration, and particularly by his taxing of church property. Also, against Gregory's wishes, an illegitimate and favorite son of Frederick's had become King of Sardinia by marriage. For the second time, Gregory excommunicated the King, on this occasion as an immoral man and a heretic.

He had some grounds for this. Frederick had moved his capital from Palermo in Sicily to Foggia. Here he was building an oriental court, with fully oriental luxury, to which princes of the Italian states sent their sons as pages to learn the social graces. Their studies, comprising literature, art, music and philosophy, derived from the writings of ancient (pagan) Rome and Greece, often in translations from the Arabic, and were an affront to rigid churchmen. So also was Frederick's private life, since he maintained a harem of concubines after the Mohammedan custom.

Frederick replied to the excommunication by sending a circular letter to the crowned heads of Europe, pointing out the dangerous

Obverse and reverse sides of gold coin issued under Frederick II

Frederick among his courtiers during a court festival in Palermo, Sicily

ambitions of the Church of Rome, and demanding that the Church reform its corrupt and licentious living. Finally, he proposed a league of temporal rulers against the Pope. As a practical measure he began to organize central Italy along the lines he had already used in Sicily and Germany.

Gregory was deeply disturbed. He summoned a synod at Rome to depose his enemy Frederick. Enzio, heading a Sardinian fleet, fought a sea battle with a Genoan convoy and captured a number of French, Spanish and Italian cardinals, bishops and priests on their way to the Synod. Frederick marched on Tuscany, which was part of the papal kingdom, and nearly captured Rome.

Gregory died, reputedly from worry and frustration. The next Pope, Celestine IX, died shortly after his election. Innocent IV was chosen, and the struggle continued. Frederick invaded Campagna, and again seemed to be in a position to capture Rome itself. Pope Innocent fled to Lyons and called a new synod, which renewed the excommunication of Frederick, imposed the same ban on all who supported him, and closed all churches in his territory. Again Frederick answered with a witty, well-composed counterblast, accusing the clergy of most of the crimes that had been alleged against him.

Pope Innocent urged the German bishops to support another claimant to the throne. The bitter war continued. Frederick set off for the north to bring help to his son Conrad. On the way he found that the Lombard people of Parma had taken the city from his garrison, and his son Enzio was in peril. He laid siege to Parma, and here made the greatest mistake of his life.

With Enzio and 50 knights he went out hawking—his favorite sport. The inhabitants of the city, both men and women, took this opportunity to rout his leaderless army. They captured Frederick's treasury, his women, and the menageries that always traveled with him. But he raised more money and a new army, and the fight grew

German aquamanile or water pitcher
from the 13th century

Frederick II, wearing a crown, leads soldiers who carry his symbol

increasingly bitter. His trusted prime minister was probably conspiring against him. His doctor, on the orders of the Pope, tried to poison him. His favorite son Enzio was captured by the people of Bologna.

Frederick, broken in spirit, retired to Apulia, in the heel of Italy. His well-trained generals carried on with considerable success. There was one curious turn of events: Louis IX of France was captured by the Sultan of Egypt during the Seventh Crusade. He appealed to the Pope to end the war with Frederick so that Frederick could free him. But this plea was in vain, for Frederick was dying of dysentery.

The last days of the King of Jerusalem, Sicily, and Emperor of the Holy Roman Empire were embittered by tragedy. Henry, his eldest and intended heir, who had twice revolted against his father, and had been captured and taken back to Italy, was still under arrest.

In 1242, while being transferred from one prison to another, he broke away from his guards and spurred his horse over a precipice, to his death.

Frederick's gallant son Enzio had also died. Perhaps an even greater blow had been the death of Piero della Vigne. Piero, trained in the law school of Bologna, had risen rapidly to become the head of Frederick's new civil service. It was Piero who had been mainly responsible for the brilliant code of laws and the honest and moderate administration. He also wrote charming poetry and was Frederick's closest friend. But after the reverses at Parma, when the whole world seemed to have turned against the King, Piero was accused of treachery. Frederick had him blinded and dragged in rags behind him, as a terrible warning to other traitors. At last, Piero dashed out his brains against the wall of his prison cell.

Did Frederick brood over the treachery of his best friend? Or did he, too late, believe that he had punished an innocent man? We know only of his retirement to Apulia. And though the tide of war had turned in his favor, he took no part in it.

In 1250 the Emperor died in Apulia. By Frederick's will his son Conrad became Emperor of the Holy Roman Empire, and King of Sicily, but with Manfred, an illegitimate son, as regent of Sicily. The Pope offered Sicily to the son of Henry III of England, renewed Conrad's excommunication, and sent a force of mercenaries against Sicily and southern Italy. And the war began again.

TERRITORY RULED BY FREDERICK II, 1250

HOLLAND

WESTPHALIA

BRUNSWICK LUNEBURG

BRANDENBURG

FRANCE

SWABIA

FRANCONIA

BOHEMIA

KINGDOM OF POLAND

SILESIA

DUCHY OF BURGUNDY

COUNTY OF BURGUNDY

BAVARIA

AUSTRIA

KINGDOM OF HUNGARY

FRANCE

KINGDOM OF BURGUNDY

Parma

BOSNIA

SERVIA

CORSICA

ELBA

Rome

ALBANIA

SICILIA

APULIA

SARDINIA

MEDITERRANEAN

Palermo

SICILY

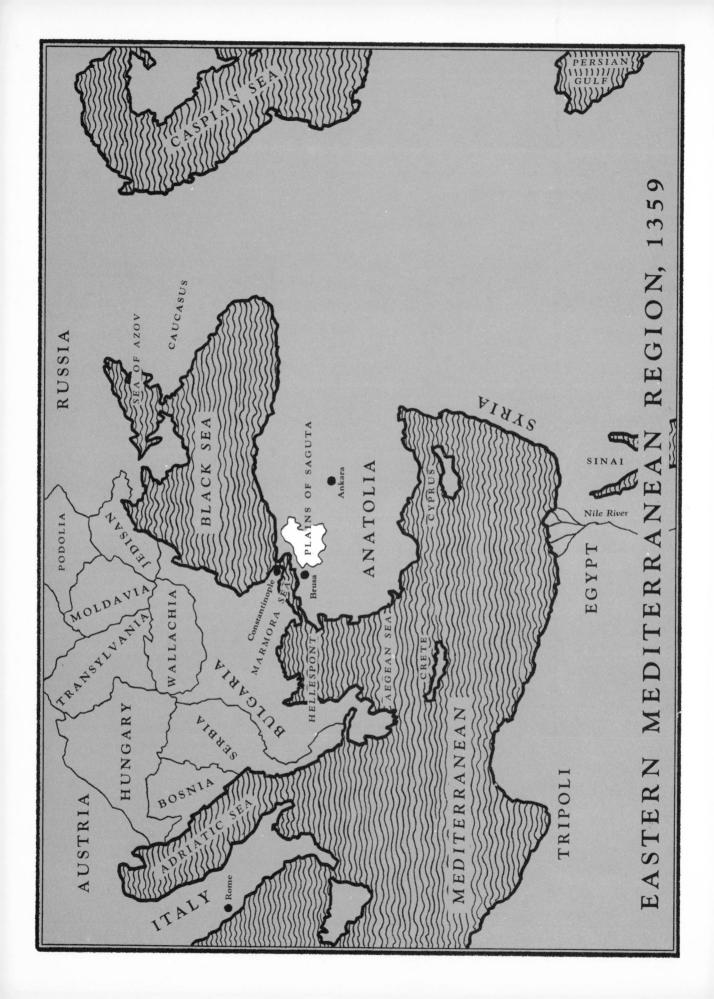

EASTERN MEDITERRANEAN REGION, 1359

RUSSIA

CASPIAN SEA

PERSIAN GULF

SEA OF AZOV

CAUCASUS

BLACK SEA

PLAINS OF SAGUTA

Ankara

ANATOLIA

SYRIA

SINAI

CYPRUS

Nile River

PODOLIA

JEDISAN

MOLDAVIA

WALLACHIA

TRANSYLVANIA

BULGARIA

Constantinople

MARMORA SEA

Brusa

HELLESPONT

AEGEAN SEA

CRETE

EGYPT

AUSTRIA

HUNGARY

SERBIA

BOSNIA

ADRIATIC SEA

MEDITERRANEAN

TRIPOLI

ITALY

Rome

The Ottoman Empire

The Ottoman Turks conquered both the Semitic lands of the the East and the Eastern Roman Empire, whose capital was Constantinople. At their height they were more powerful than either. Their base was in Anatolia—now Turkey—but for centuries they held all southeastern Europe in subjection. Until 1914, Syria, Palestine, Iraq, Arabia, and Egypt were all part of the vast Ottoman Empire.

The small and impoverished Turkish clan that achieved this remarkable feat originally consisted of some unimportant nomad families who had been driven out of Central Asia by the Mongols. Arriving in Anatolia, they were given land by the Seljuks, another Turkish people who ruled the area. Like the Arabs, they were Moslems, but the civilized Arabs nevertheless scorned them as barbarians; and the Christians of the Byzantine Empire scorned them as both barbarians and Moslems.

Many historians trying to account for the subsequent triumph of the Ottoman Empire have stressed the decadence of both the Islamic and Byzantine Empires, and the inability of the European peoples in the Balkans to settle the quarrels they had among themselves. These circumstances, it is argued, made it easy for the Turks to defeat the Arabs and the Christians. But the fierce warfare the Ottoman Turks had to wage, generation after generation, to establish their empire contradicts the theory of an easy takeover. In fact, there were many reasons for the Ottoman triumph, and not all of them had to do with the weakness or decadence of their enemies. Chief among these reasons was the fact that the Turks were, by tradition, excellent warriors and that they were blessed by a series of remarkable leaders.

In their homeland in Asia, these nomadic herdsmen had been thinly spread over vast, unfertile areas. When they needed land they

Mohammed II, Sultan of Turkey,
and Conqueror of the Great

could gather enough warriors to raid a neighboring clan, but they could not keep enough fighting men in reserve to repel a similar attack on themselves by another clan. Their safety lay in striking first. By slaughtering the men of a nearby village and capturing its women, children, and livestock, they weakened all of their potential enemies. In such conditions, the Ottomans did not have to worry about defending themselves, but they did have to live in a state of constant warfare. Every man and every boy in his teens was a tough warrior—he had to be if the clan was to survive. The cold semidesert of central Asia produced the Turks who sparked the Ottoman conquests, just as the hot semidesert of Arabia produced the Bedouins who achieved the Islamic conquests. To both of these peoples warfare was only an enlarged and more profitable form of the small tribal raids their ancestors had carried on. Aside from being fierce and able warriors, the Ottomans managed to choose capable leaders. The first of these was a man named Osman.

Osman (or Othman) 1288–1326

Osman was the son of Ertogrul, the first man who can be said to have ruled the entire tribe. He had been given land for his people near Ankara by the Sultan of the Seljuk clan of Turks. Ertogrul died in 1289, having established his authority over the other chiefs of the clan and repelled a Tartar invasion of his territory. He was succeeded by his son Osman, who immediately declared his independence from the Seljuks.

This made him the leader of an independent empire. He wished to add new territory, and this brought him into conflict with Byzantium and the Eastern Roman Empire, a conflict that was to last for over 200 years. In his first clash with the Byzantines, he took Bithynia and laid siege to Brusa. The siege was unsuccessful but, by setting up headquarters nearby, Osman pinned down the Byzantine troops within the city walls. From this base he fought off a force of Tartar raiders, defeated them, and converted them to Islam. He then gave them land and added them to his small but growing army. After a long siege Osman's son, Orkhan took Brusa for him. Osman died in 1326, after uniting his conquered territories under an effective military government. He gave his name, Osman or Othman, to his clan, who became known as Osmanlis and later Ottomans.

Orkhan 1326–59

Appointed as successor by his father, Orkhan, the conqueror of Brusa, was quickly acclaimed as leader by the clan. It was Orkhan who first organized the administration of what was to become the Ottoman Empire. His first act was to make his elder brother vizier, or prime minister. Orkhan as chief, or Emir, ruled as commander in chief of the armies, and the vizier was his administrator for civil affairs. But civil government among the Osmanlis was still fairly simple, with the people obeying the religious laws of Mohammed and following many of their own ancient customs. So the vizier, like the Emir, was often free to lead troops in combat.

The Osmanlis were no longer simple herdsmen but warriors, conquerors, and statesmen. Orkhan's government began to build roads, mint money, and establish schools to teach the religion and religious

Made of silver and iron, this Turkish warrior's helmet is like those worn by Orkhan's soldiers

Turkish saber, known as a "scimitar," has jade hilt and jeweled scabbard

laws of Mohammed. Already the Osmanli army included Tartars, Seljuks, Semites, and Greeks. The Mohammedan religion united these different races in a common purpose—to spread Islam by the sword and, if Allah willed it, to die in battle and be certain of Paradise.

When Orkhan became Emir he was already an experienced general, and he showed sound judgement in the first crisis that faced him. The Seljuk Emirs to the south and east of Brusa refused to acknowledge one of their members who had declared himself Sultan. Civil war broke out, presenting Orkhan with a tempting opportunity to move in and take over while the Seljuks fought among themselves. But he wisely chose to remain at Brusa, his new capital, and strengthen his position. From there he could extend his conquests over the nearby Byzantine territories.

Even after Orkhan had established a strong base at Brusa, the Seljuks were still fighting among themselves. This time, Orkhan was free to seize the opportunity. He laid siege to the old Seljuk city of Nicaea and captured it in 1331. Almost the whole of northern Anatolia, up to the southern shore of the Sea of Marmora, was now in his hands.

Orkhan's unbroken string of successes alarmed Constantinople. Andronicus III, the Byzantine Emperor, led an army south across the Bosphorus, determined to crush the Osmanlis before they grew more powerful. Andronicus and Orkhan met, each personally leading his troops. Orkhan wounded the Emperor in the hand, won the battle, and went on to take the Byzantine city of Nicomedia in 1337.

In seven years Orkhan and his Osmanlis had overrun more land and conquered more people than they needed or could govern. The Emir parceled out wide estates among his chiefs and allies in exchange for their promise to furnish him with horsemen and foot soldiers. The harsh rule of the Osmanlis also applied to these territories; inhabitants who chose not to accept Islam had no legal rights and could be robbed, raped, or slaughtered at will by the Mohammed soldiery.

With such absolute power in the territories they had won, most armies of occupation would have settled down and turned their energies from conquest to civilization. The Emir foresaw that this might happen and, since he was not ready to end his conquests, took steps to prevent it. He ordered that one-fifth of the Christian boys captured as slaves and converted to Islam be handed over to him. He put them in barracks, fed them, gave them an excellent education, and trained them in the strictest military discipline. This was the beginning of the palace guard, the corps of Janizaries (from two Turkish words meaning "new soldiers"), who were to play a leading role in establishing and maintaining the Ottoman Empire by military force. Later emirs exacted a tribute of boys in addition to the tax from all of the subject races in the Balkans. This steady supply of recruits, all possessing the fanatical zeal of new converts, kept alive the aggressive spirit of the early Osmanlis. Unlike the other troops, the Janizaries received regular pay. They became the core of the Ottoman army. But later, when they began to mix in politics, they became one of the main causes of its decay.

The Osmanlis and their Emir knew only one respectable occupation—warfare. And the Byzantine Empire soon offered them an opportunity. Andronicus III was dead, and his son Palaeologos ascended the throne as John V. He was still a minor and his mother had to act as regent for him. The Mayor of the Imperial Palace John Cantacuzene, set out to overthrow the young Emperor, and asked Orkhan to help him to do so. Orkhan obliged by sending his son Suleiman at the head of a small Turkish force. Suleiman crossed the Hellespont with only 80 men on three makeshift rafts. They captured a fort on the European side and seized enough craft to ferry over 4,000 more troops. After capturing the major Byzantine fort at Gallipoli, Suleiman advanced further into the Balkans, crushing the enemies of John Cantacuzene who had remained loyal to the young Emperor. But here John's treachery backfired. He paid Orkhan to hand over the captured territories, but Orkhan, after taking the money, refused to give up the land.

The adventure into the Balkans had been a gamble, and succeeded only because the Mayor and the Emperor were at odds with one another. But as a result of the gamble, the Osmanlis now held land on each side of the enormously rich and famous city of Constantinople. Orkhan cast covetous eyes on the city, but he was a calculating gen-

Armor made of plate and mail protected Turkish soldiers from swords and arrows

eral, not an impulsive upstart. He knew that the high, fortressed walls of Constantinople had withstood armies many times stronger than his. So he recalled Suleiman and his troops to Asia Minor and proceeded with the conquest of the lands to the east, which were held by the Tartars.

Suleiman, Orkhan's son and intended successor, died from a fall from his horse in 1359. Orkhan died two months later, perhaps of grief at his son's death, and Murad, his second son, succeeded him as Emir.

Murad (or Amurath) 1359–89

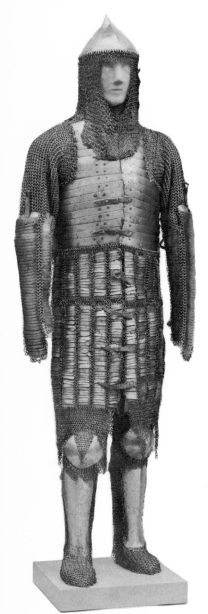

Though less famous than his brother Suleiman, Murad, at age 41, was already an experienced leader. This was fortunate, for he was barely acclaimed Emir before he had to face a new enemy, the Turkomans. The Turkomans, though long settled in Iran, were a distant branch of the same Turks from whom the Osmanlis were descended. In a series of major raids, they had swept westward and captured Ankara, where Murad's great-grandfather Ertogrul had been granted land by the Seljuk Sultan. Considering their recent gains in Europe, the Osmanlis were not too disturbed by the loss of Ankara. But they were dangerously extended from northwest to southeast, and their hold on Europe was too insecure to risk any weakening of their base in Asia Minor. Moreover, the Turkoman victories had affronted their tribal pride. So in 1361 Murad collected a large army, regained Ankara, and drove off the Turkomans.

But there was another weakness in the Osmanli position: their territory was split into two parts, European and Asiatic, by Byzantium. This strategic weakness was to plague the Osmanli Emirs for 200 years. At whatever end of the empire the army happened to be, trouble would break out on the other end and the army would have to march back to deal with it. This time, Murad had barely dealt with the Tartars when problems arose at Constantinople.

His father Orkhan had sided with John Cantacuzene against the Emperor John V. Cantacuzene had gone on to overthrow the young

Ottoman suit of iron was worn by conquering warriors during the 1400's

Emperor and rule as John VI. But John V had regained his power, and now Cantacuzene was dead. Understandably enough, John V wished to punish the Osmanlis who had helped to overthrow him. Murad had to make a choice—peace or war. To make peace with his father's enemy would be taken as a sign of weakness, so in 1361 he declared war. He marched his army north again, extended his conquests over Byzantine territory and, in 1365, took Adrianople, the second capital of the Byzantine Empire.

In the meantime he had captured the town of Philippopolis in Bulgaria, and the Christian Serbs, Bulgarians, Wallachians, and Moldavians began to realize their danger. They forgot their differences and united to drive out the Moslem Turks. The Moslems defeated them and proceeded to raid the borders of Albania and Greece. Meanwhile, Murad secured his hold on Adrianople and in 1367 made it his capital in place of Brusa.

Impressed by the remains of Roman civilization that he saw at Adrianople, Murad determined to build a capital to equal the Roman cities and thereby to emphasize the fact that he was in Europe to stay.

Meanwhile, John V repaired the walls of Constantinople and waited for the inevitable Turkish attack. For centuries the Imperial City had been besieged and assaulted by hosts of Avars, Arabs, Bulgarians, and crusaders from the West. All of these enemies had come and gone, but the city still stood. The Emperor felt that Byzantium could wait while these new Osmanli pests bled themselves to death with constant battles. Then, as so often before, the Empire would recover all her lost possessions—or so thought John V.

No formal peace was made between the aggressive-minded Osmanlis and the defensive-minded Byzantines, but a wary diplomatic friendship grew up between the Emir and the Emperor. The Emperor gave one of his daughters in marriage to Murad, and two more to Murad's sons. On occasion one of the Emperor's sons served with the Osmanli troops in order to gain military experience. But the only time the Emperor himself ventured outside the city walls was when he sailed down the Dardanelles to seek help from Pope Urban V and King Charles V of France. Since the Emperor belonged to the Orthodox Church of the Eastern Empire, the Catholics of the West considered him a heretic and little better than the infidel Turk who threatened him. His mission was not very successful.

While Murad and his main army were in the north subduing rebellions among the Balkan peoples, trouble again broke out in the south. Sauji, the Emir's oldest son, had been left to hold Brusa, the old capital in Asia Minor. With the help of Andronicus, a son of John V of Byzantium, Sauji defeated an attack against that city. Elated by their success, the two sons conspired to overthrow their fathers. The revolt failed, for as soon as Murad appeared with his army, the troops of Sauji and Andronicus deserted them. Sauji was put to death for treason, and Andronicus was blinded, according to Byzantine custom. Murad went on to defeat the Seljuks again, this time at Konia, some 150 miles south of Ankara.

Because Murad had been called south, the Bosnians in the north had seized the opportunity to drive Murad's governor out of Rumelia. Heartened by this success, the King of Serbia revolted. Hurrying back north, Murad first defeated the King of Bulgaria, then marched on to meet the Serbian King, who headed a force of 100,000 Serbians, Hungarians, Moldavians, and Wallachians. Murad defeated them at the Battle of Kossovo in 1389. While he was reviewing his troops after the battle, a wounded Serbian rose up and knifed him. Murad died, and the King of Serbia, who had been taken prisoner, was killed in reprisal. Murad was carried back to be buried with his ancestors in Brusa.

Bayezid (or Bajazed) 1389–1403

Bayezid, Murad's oldest son, succeeded his father. His first act as Emir was to execute his brother Yakub Chelebi. The simple days when the Emir could appoint his brother as his prime minister and work with him in trust and amity were over.

The new Emir had scarcely assumed command when certain intrigues occurred in Constantinople to strengthen his position. Andronicus, the Emperor's son who had been blinded for rebellion, recovered partial sight in one eye. He offered Bayezid 30,000 ducats to

Woven design from Byzantine Empire indicates past richness of that state

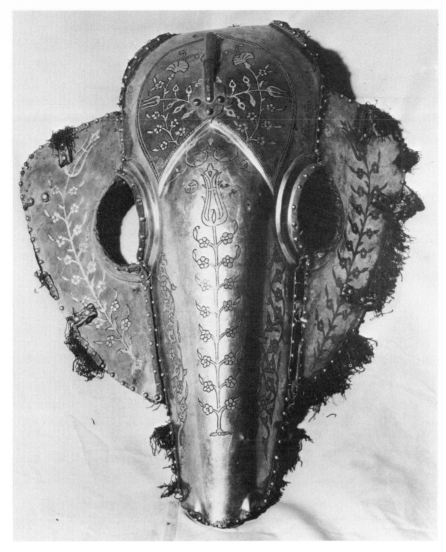

Weird frontal armor protected horses of the Turks during fierce battles

help him avenge himself on his father. But his father got wind of the offer and offered to give Bayezid an equal amount of money, plus 12,000 soldiers, to withhold his support from Andronicus. Bayezid accepted the higher offer.

One result of this deal was that when Bayezid began to extend his conquests westward toward the Aegean Sea, Manuel, a son of the Emperor, accompanied the Osmanlis at the head of the 12,000 Byzantine troops. Bayezid used his new auxiliaries in the storming of the fortress of Ala Shehr. From there Bayezid turned south to subdue the leaders of the Karamanians.

That, of course, was the signal for trouble in the north. This time it was the Wallachians who revolted. Bayezid rushed north again and defeated them. Then he had to force march south again, for the recently subdued Karamanians had risen against him. Bayezid put down that rebellion and captured the nearby Tartar towns of Kaisarieh, Sivas, and Tokat, thus strengthening his eastern border.

Constant marching, sieges, and battles, against a variety of races and using a variety of weapons and tactics, kept Bayezid and his men in good fighting form. These battles also rewarded the soldiers with loot and slaves and replenished Bayezid's treasury.

Still, the powerful Ottoman army had not managed to take Constantinople. Every time they passed from north to south or south to north, they had to march almost under the walls of the city. It became increasingly clear that the Imperial City was the key to Bayezid's strategic problem, for it divided his Empire. The fabulously rich metropolis was more than a tempting prize. It was the obvious future capital of the Ottoman Empire, from which the Emir could control both the Balkans and Asia Minor.

John V, the Byzantine Emperor, died in 1390. His son Manuel, who had helped Bayezid capture Ala Shehr, received the news and thought it prudent to escape from the Osmanli army. He reached Constantinople and was immediately proclaimed Emperor.

If Bayezid had detained Manuel, another emperor would have been elected and Bayezid would then have had the choice of supporting Manuel's claim, holding him hostage, or killing him. Any of these acts would have started trouble in Constantinople and weakened Byzantine rule. Bayezid had missed his chance.

But a good general does not depend solely on chance opportunities. If no opportunities arise, he makes his own. Now was the time for Bayezid's next move. For the moment, both the south and the north had been beaten into helplessness. Summoning all his available forces, he began to lay siege to Constantinople in 1391. While he kept the best part of the Byzantine army pinned down behind the famous city walls, he drove west to seize the Byzantine territories in Thessaly and Macedonia. He was besieging the rich port of Thessalonica (Salonica) when disturbing news came from the north.

Victorious Ottoman troops are shown in this 16th-century painting

Glazed earthenware plate, decorated in blue and green, was produced by Turkish civilization during 1400's

THE METROPOLITAN MUSEUM

A force of 100,000 crusaders had driven south through Hungary, Transylvania, and Wallachia, gathering support from the Christians as they advanced. They had crossed the Danube unopposed and laid siege to Nikopolis, the seat of Osmanli rule in Bulgaria.

This forced Bayezid to abandon his operations in Thessaly and Macedonia and withdraw his troops from under the walls of Constantinople. He reached Nikopolis, just in time to save it. With an estimated force of 60,000 men he defeated the more numerous Christian forces and killed them almost to the last man. Then he returned to resume the siege of Constantinople.

But Bayezid's forces were simply not strong enough to break the heavy defenses of the city, and the siege had become largely a bluff. At length, the Emir allowed himself to be bought off by Emperor Manuel. But this was a bad move on Manuel's part, for it allowed Bayezid to concentrate all his forces in Thessaly and bring that region more firmly under his control. Once he had done that, he could steadily weaken the Byzantine Empire by harrassing it from the east and from the west. It is possible that during the next few years Bayezid might have worn down and conquered the Byzantines. But something unexpected happened to prevent him from following this course.

Far off to the east, almost on the borders of China, a general even greater than Bayezid was on the march. His name was Timur Leng

(Timur the Lame or Tamurlane). A Moslem Tartar and the great-great-grandson of the famous Genghis Khan, Timur had fought his way to power as ruler of Samarkand. In 1398 he had invaded India, sacked the huge city of Delhi and returned home with incredibly rich booty. In his next campaign he had captured in rapid succession the Arabic cities of Baghdad, Aleppo, and Damascus from the Islamic Empire. Now he was on the Osmanlis' eastern frontier in Asia Minor.

There was no choice. Once again Bayezid had to leave unfinished the task of conquering the Byzantines and attend to this new menace. Timur demanded that Bayezid grant independence to the Seljuk and Tartar territories the Osmanlis had subjugated in Asia Minor. Bayezid, who had never lost a battle before, was confident of success and rejected Timur's demand. In 1402 the Tartar and Osmanli armies met near Ankara.

As in the great battle between Bayezid and the crusaders at Nikopolis, the Osmanlis were outnumbered by about two to one. The Tartars, however, were just as brave and much more disciplined than the crusaders. The result was a crushing defeat for the Osmanlis. Bayezid's eldest son and intended successor fell in the battle. To ensure that the Osmanlis would have a leader under whom they could unite their Empire, Bayezid ordered his Vizier to escape with the youngest son Suleiman. Bayezid himself was captured, and Timur received him as an honored guest. But, as the victor's guest, he had to undergo the humiliating experience of seeing Timur capture Brusa, which held the Osmanli treasure, and then Nicaea. This, along with the loss of his oldest son, is said to have plunged him into a despondency from which he died in 1403. Timur went on to capture most of Asia Minor before returning to the east. He died in 1405, just as he was about to start on an even more ambitious campaign, the invasion of China.

Disorganization 1402–13

The rout of the Osmanli forces was complete; the sons of Bayezid fled, offering no resistance to Timur. Timur, having freed the Tartar and Seljuk territories, made no attempt to cross over into Europe, but sent messages to Bayezid's sons giving them back their father's possessions, minus the areas he had freed.

What remained of the Ottoman Empire was now divided between two of Bayezid's sons. Mohammed defeated his brother Musa and became ruler of the remaining Asiatic possessions; Suleiman became ruler of the European possessions. Suleiman crossed into Anatolia and defeated Mohammed, but did not establish control over the Asiatic territories. Mohammed regained his rule and Suleiman, returning to Anatolia to defeat Mohammed again, was captured and strangled. Mohammed now took control of the whole Empire.

Mohammed 1413–21

Mohammed, as ruler of both Asia Minor and the European territories, was the first Emir (or Sultan, as the leader was now called) of the Osmanli Empire since the death of his father Bayezid. He recaptured Konia from the Karamanians in 1416, turned north to defeat the Wallachians, and re-established Osmanli control in the Balkans by building schools and encouraging literature. By the time of his death in 1421 he had regained all the Osmanli Empire and, with a view to future extension or as a threat to Constantinople, had begun to build a navy.

Slender nosepiece on this gilded helmet could be lowered for additional protection

Murad II 1421–51

Murad, Mohammed's son, was a young man when he succeeded his father, but he was scarcely inexperienced. At 12 years of age, he had been entrusted by Mohammed with the command of 60,000 confidence of a full 18 years, he was ready to defy the Byzantine men to suppress a revolt among the Osmanlis. Now, with the self-Emperor, Manuel II.

A man who called himself Mustapha—and who closely resembled Bayezid's eldest son, who was also called Mustapha and had died in the Battle of Ankara—attempted to seize the sultanate from Mohammed. Defeated, he fled for protection to Manuel II. The Emperor refused to hand him over to Mohammed, but, for a large annual payment, had agreed to keep him safely out of mischief.

Murad, when he became Sultan, refused to continue these payments. Manuel responded by freeing Mustapha, who left the island of Lemnos, landed in Gallipoli and, gathering adherents, marched north and seized Adrianople. His success brought him more supporters. He marched south and crossed the Dardanelles to meet Murad's troops, who were marching north to oppose him. As soon as the armies approached each other, Mustapha's commanding general defected with all his troops to the army of Murad. Mustapha tried to escape by sea, but was captured and put to death.

Before long, another man named Mustapha appeared to threaten Murad's authority. This time it was Murad's own brother. This Mustapha, however, was only a young boy of 13, who was probably being used by Murad's enemies. The boy was betrayed to Murad, who had him put to death.

In 1426 Murad made a hasty peace with the Kermians and Karamanians whom he had been fighting, and resumed the Osmanli siege of Constantinople. The death of Manuel II in 1425 brought John Palaeologos (John VIII) to the Byzantine throne. Previously, emperors had demanded money of the Osmanli. But the Emperor realized that the Osmanli had become stronger while the Byzantine position had grown weaker. He offered to pay Murad a heavy tribute and cede to him all the Byzantine possessions except for two towns on the Black Sea, if Murad would call off the siege of Constantinople. Now, for the first time since Timur had seized the Osmanli gold at Brusa during the reign of Bayezid, the Osmanlis had enough money to take the initiative against Byzantium.

Thessaly, part of the Byzantine Empire until Murad's father had conquered it, had become feebly independent under the protection of the Venetians, who were expanding their trade and influence eastward from Italy. Murad stormed the capital of Thessaly at Thessalonica, which was held by only a small garrison of 1,500 Venetians, and allowed his troops to butcher and enslave the inhabitants. Constantinople could do nothing to save its former subjects.

Murad had shown that the Byzantines could not defend their territory beyond the gates of the Imperial City. But now the old game began anew. Once more a Karamanian revolt called Murad back to Asia Minor. Again he had to make hasty peace terms with these rebels, for a more serious threat had developed in the north. In 1422 an enemy coalition had captured Hermanstadt (Sibiu) in Hungary and had pressed down as far south as Semendria, near the present city of Belgrade. Murad laid siege to Belgrade, but the siege was broken by enemy cannon fire. The Osmanlis had never faced cannon before and were terrified. The all-conquering Osmanlis were shaken in morale, and soon after were heavily defeated by the Rumanian general Hunniades. In 1444, Murad was forced to sign a ten-year peace with Hungary.

Murad was now only 41 years old, but he seemed to have lost his enthusiasm for combat. Shortly after the defeat at Belgrade, he retired to private life, appointing his young son Mohammed II as his successor. The news of Murad's retirement brought the Hungarians and Wallachians out in force, and they were urged on by Pope Eugenius IV, who preached a crusade against the Turks. Murad came hastily out of retirement and defeated the Hungarians at Varna on the Black Sea in November 1444. Soon after this he was called out again, this time to put down a revolt of the Janizaries. He seemed to have recovered his enthusiasm, for in 1446 he conquered much of what is now Greece and in 1448 defeated the Hungarians at the second battle of Kossovo. In 1451, Murad died in his northern capital at Adrianople.

Mohammed II triumphantly enters the conquered city of Constantinople

Mohammed II (the Conqueror) 1451–81

When his father died, Mohammed was just 21 years old. With youthful energy, Mohammed began by suppressing yet another Karamanian revolt, and by the year 1453, was reaching for the grand prize—the rich and famous city of Constantinople.

For nearly a century every Osmanli leader had coveted the city. Bayezid had tried to gamble for it, but Timur had wrecked his hopes. Murad II could almost certainly have taken it, but only at heavy cost. Barring unforeseen difficulties, such as the appearance of another enemy like Timur, the new Sultan was confident that he would succeed where his predecessors had failed.

This time, the defenders of Constantinople would face a new enemy—cannon. Eighteen years before, at the siege of Belgrade, the

Mohammed II was called
Conqueror of the Great

Osmanlis had been broken by this new weapon. Since then, they had bought guns and powder and had trained the Janizaries in their use. The weapon which the Christians had used to rout the Moslems would now be used against the greatest of the Christian cities. In addition, Mohammed had called up the strongest force of cavalry archers, foot soldiers, and military engineers the Osmanlis had ever known—almost 150,000 men.

On April 7, 1453, Mohammed cut off Constantinople on every side, by water as well as by land, and commenced the siege.

Constantine Palaeologos, ruler of all that was left of the once proud Eastern Roman Empire, had long realized that his position was desperate. Four years before the siege he had made a last attempt to get help from the Catholics of the West against the Moslems. He had renounced his Orthodox faith and had embraced Catholicism, but even this had not moved the Pope and the other Catholic leaders. Instead, the gesture had cost him the support of his Orthodox subjects, some of whom spoke openly of unconditional surrender to the Turks. Later, some of these discontented Byzantines tried to betray the city to the Turks, for it was the custom of war in those times to deal lightly with an enemy who surrendered after only token resistance.

Even the historic city walls were a source of weakness to the defenders, for they ran for so many miles that the small Byzantine garrison was spread much too thin. The city was stocked with enough food and water for a long siege, but it was nevertheless a dispirited guard that closed and reinforced the gates.

But just before the siege guns began to roar, help came from the West. The merchants of Genoa sent a small force of ships with about 500 well-armed soldiers to aid the Byzantines. These men became the very heart of the defense.

Mohammed pounded the defences set on the land side with 14 batteries of cannon, but without great effect. By clearing away the houses of Galata, outside the city walls, he hauled 60 ships overland into the harbor of Constantinople and furnished them with huge rock launchers and wooden towers for archers and musketeers. But despite the weakness of the defenses facing the harbor, the Genoese force held off the attack.

The defense was hopeless. The end came on the night of May 29, 1453. During the day the Osmanlic cannon had made a breach in the walls. The Genoese commander was engaged in closing the gap with a wooden barricade when he was wounded and had to retire to have the wound dressed. In his absence the defense crumbled. Mohammed ordered forward a detachment of his disciplined Janizaries, who stormed the barricade and killed Constantine. The last Emperor of the Byzantines died sword in hand. Constantinople, the Imperial City that had withstood the Turks for so long, fell to them at last.

A century of continual fighting, ruthless conquest, and cunning diplomacy had forged the last link in the Ottoman Empire. With Constantinople as a strategic center, Mohammed now extended his power from the Crimea to the heel of Italy. His successors were able

Turkish pistol is from the 19th century, later years of the Ottoman Empire

to double the size of the Empire, conquering Syria, Palestine, Arabia, Iraq, and Egypt. Having conquered these lands, which had belonged to the Islamic Empire, the Ottoman Sultan was able to declare himself Kahlif, the religious head of Islam and representative on earth of the Prophet Mohammed.

The decline of the Ottoman Empire followed the usual course of successful despotisms. Once they were free of the necessity for conquest, the Sultans became corrupted by luxury and absolute power. They grew weak, and a weak ruler can trust no one. One Sultan executed no less than twelve of his viziers. Other Sultans murdered their brothers or sons rather than risk their competition for the throne. Even a Sultan's intended heir was regarded with suspicion and kept a prisoner in the palace, where he learned nothing of the arts of war or administration. The corps of Janizaries, now the only well-trained fighting men in the Empire, took to politics and became unreliable. The administration became so corrupt that power and justice were no longer administered, but bought and sold.

In a series of wars in the eighteenth and nineteenth centuries, the Ottoman Empire was shorn of its European territories. Finally, it lost Syria, Palestine, Arabia, Iraq, and Egypt. Pruned back to modern Turkey, its capital removed from cosmopolitan Constantinople to Ankara in 1919. Here Ertogrul had first settled with his small clan of nomads, Osmanli Empire ceased being an Empire and became a nation, less powerful than the surrounding nations it had once ruled.

But the glory of the Osmanlis is to be found in the days when, under a remarkable succession of leaders, they challenged and finally conquered the Byzantine Empire.

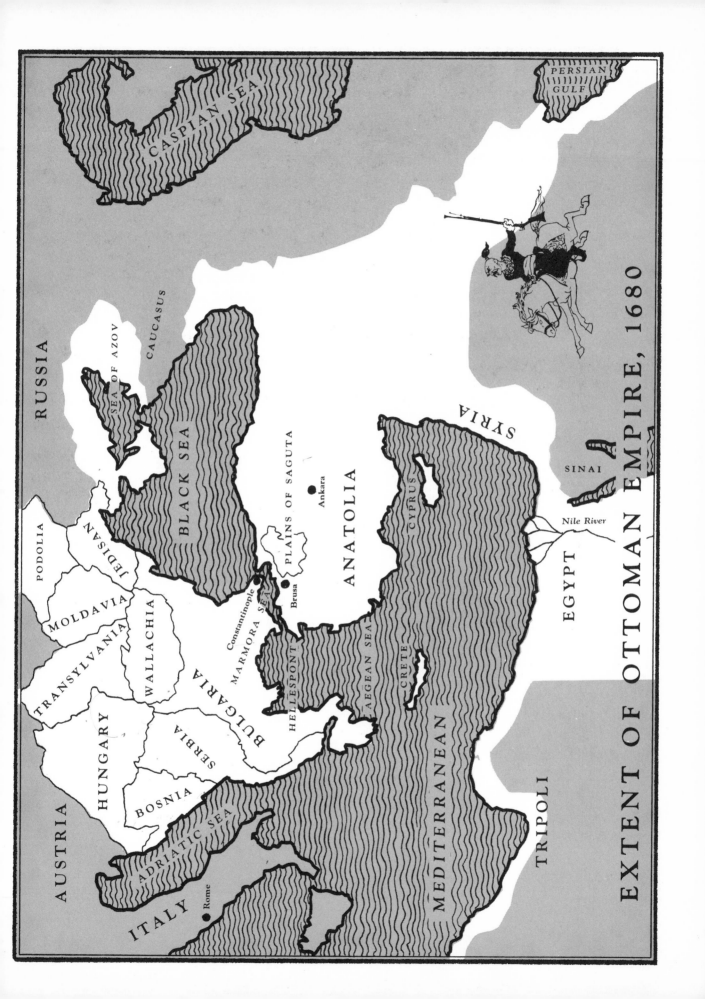

RUSSIA

CASPIAN SEA

PERSIAN
GULF

SEA OF AZOV

CAUCASUS

BLACK SEA

SYRIA

PODOLIA

JEDISAN

SINAI

MOLDAVIA

WALLACHIA

PLAINS OF SAGUTA

ANATOLIA

CYPRUS

Nile River

TRANSYLVANIA

BULGARIA

Constantinople

MARMORA SEA

Brusa

Ankara

EGYPT

AUSTRIA

HUNGARY

SERBIA

HELLESPONT

AEGEAN SEA

CRETE

MEDITERRANEAN

TRIPOLI

BOSNIA

ADRIATIC SEA

ITALY   • Rome

EXTENT OF OTTOMAN EMPIRE, 1680

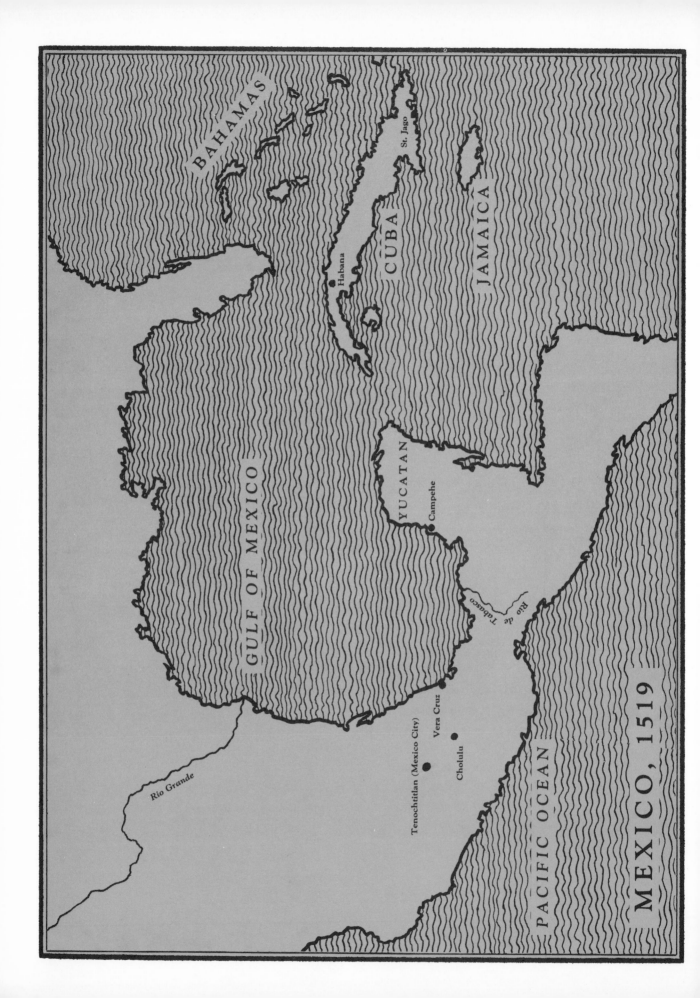

BAHAMAS

CUBA

St. Jago

Habana

JAMAICA

YUCATAN

Campehe

GULF OF MEXICO

Rio de Tabasco

Tenochtitlan (Mexico City)

Vera Cruz

Cholula

Rio Grande

PACIFIC OCEAN

MEXICO, 1519

Hernando Cortes

In the years following Columbus's discovery of the New World in 1492, there was a great wave of European exploration in Central and South America. At first, most sailors thought that Columbus had only touched on the eastern shores of Asia, or perhaps the Spice Islands off Asia. But when it became clear that Columbus had really discovered a new world, one not even shown on the maps of the day, the rulers of Europe began to dream of conquest and gold, and to send explorers to report on the newly discovered lands.

The first government to undertake large-scale exploration was that of Spain. It was the Spanish King Ferdinand with his Queen Isabella who had financed the voyage of Columbus. They and their successors continued to send out expeditions throughout the sixteenth century, until Spain had become ruler of most of South America and much of North America.

In 1518, when the unpopular Charles I, grandson of Ferdinand and Isabella, came to the throne of Spain, the new lands to the west had already been explored from the central coast of South America to the northern part of Central America. Explorers had climbed the barrier hills of the Isthmus of Panama; Balboa had penetrated into North America and discovered the Pacific Ocean; Hispaniola—the large island that now contains Haiti and the Dominican Republic—had been colonized by Spain. But the lands off the great Gulf of Mexico still lay waiting for exploration. The rich gold and silver mines of Mexico were yet to be exploited by the Europeans and the Indians who guarded them were yet to be conquered.

In the lands already conquered, settlements, plantations, and even towns had been established. The Indians had been subdued and made to work on the plantations of the Europeans. Many of them had been

Hernando Cortes, Spanish explorer and conquistador

persuaded, or forced, to abandon their gods and accept the Christian religion of their conquerors. Though Queen Isabella of Spain had forbidden slavery, she was not able to prevent its use by her colonists in the New World.

The conquest of Mexico was to follow much the same pattern. The Aztecs and Mayans, who ruled much of the territory, fought the Europeans more fiercely than the Indians of the countries previously conquered, but in the end they too were subdued and their civilization destroyed.

The exploration of Mexico began in a small way in 1517, when a Spanish nobleman, sailing from Cuba to a neighboring island in search of slaves, was blown off course and landed on the shore of Yucatan. He set out to explore the land along the coast, and met with fierce opposition from the Mayan warriors who inhabited the area. But he and his men did stay long enough to discover that the Mayans were a civilized people, with strong stone buildings, gorgeous clothing, and a proud, warlike bearing. This surprised the Spaniards because these Indians were so different from the uncivilized tribes of the islands, with their rough, mud huts and their utter inability to defend themselves. Had the Spaniards landed a few centuries earlier, they would have been even more impressed, since by 1517, the Mayan civilization was in its death throes.

The news of the rich Mayan civilization, and the possibility that even greater riches lay beyond, excited the greed of Diego Velasquez, the conqueror and Governor of Cuba. He sent out an expedition to Yucatan, choosing one of the plantation owers in Cuba as its captain. This met with little success, but it served to sharpen Velasquez' desire to penetrate further into this rich land and to conquer it. He began to build vessels for a new expedition and to look for a leader.

He first chose Juan de Grijalva, an honest man who was perhaps too honest to be a successful conqueror. Grijalva landed in lower Mexico and claimed the territory for the Crown, calling it New Spain. But he did not conquer the territory, though he did return to Cuba with enough gold to excite further the greed of Velasquez. Velasquez was not satisfied with a few gold trinkets, however. He wanted more, and began to search for a leader who could bring it to him.

His attention fell on a young man 32 years of age, who had already helped conquer what is now Nicaragua. The young man's name was Hernando Cortes.

Cortes, the son of an ancient and respectable family, was born in Medellin, Spain in 1485. At 14 he was sent to the University of Salamanca to study law. But young Cortes wanted adventure, not study, and returned home after two years at the university with little more than a smattering of Latin and an ability to make pretty verses. After leaving the university, he spent his days in idleness, resenting the discipline of study and work. When he reached 17, his parents proposed that he join an expedition headed for Hispaniola. But an accident prevented him from doing this. He was visiting a lady one night, when part of the wall he was climbing to reach her chambers fell on him. The resulting brain concussion kept him home for another two years.

In 1504, a small squadron captained by Alonso Quintera was being outfitted for a voyage to the Caribbean. Cortes joined the expedition and reached Hispaniola in the same year. There he presented himself to the governor, who offered him a grant of land. But to

Map, drawn by Vespucci in early 1500's, shows Old and New Worlds

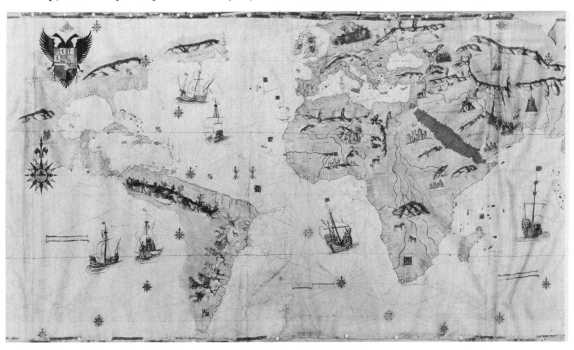

Bound for Mexico, Cortes's fleet sails out of the harbor at St. Jago

make a fortune from planting would take several years, and the hot-blooded young adventurer did not wish to wait that long. In 1511, he joined Diego Velasquez in the conquest of Cuba. Velasquez remembered him from that campaign and, after much deliberation, chose him to lead a new expedition to the Gulf of Mexico. Cortes had already proven himself a man of courage, and now, as a landowner, he could contribute money to help finance the expedition. Cortes was so enthralled by the vast riches and honor he saw before him that he mortgaged his estates in Cuba and persuaded several of his friends to invest in the enterprise.

An expeditionary force of 11 ships, 600 men, 17 horses and 10 cannon was organized. They embarked at the little town of St. Jago, Cuba on November 18, 1518. Cortes, already a seasoned and dedi-

cated leader at age 33, was in command. They stopped in Trini-
dad for some weeks to take on supplies, then sailed westward toward
New Spain. But one of the captains, landing before Cortes, looted
the Indian temples and so frightened the natives that they fled. This
greatly displeased Cortes, for he had hoped to make a peaceful treaty
with the natives and convert them to Christianity.

Coasting along the shores of Campehe, the squadron put in at the
bay of Rio de Tabasco. Here they met with fierce opposition, but,
aided by their horses and superior weapons, overcame it. After yield-
ing to the Spaniards, the Indians gave them gifts of gold and slaves.
Cortes was presented with a slave girl whom the Mayans had captured from the Aztecs to the west. Her name was Marina (Ma-
linche); she was a chief's daughter and spoke both Mayan and Aztec.
Later, when she had learned Spanish as well, she was to prove an invaluable interpreter for the Spaniards.

Sailing on Holy Thursday, 1519, Cortes landed his men, horses,
and cannon near what is now Vera Cruz and immediately set up
palisades for defense. The natives were awed by the white men, and
particularly by their horses, which they had never seen before. For
a long time, the natives of the New World thought that the rider
and the horse were part of the same animal. It took them some time
to discover that the rider, without his horse, was only a man, no
stronger than themselves.

Cortes told the chief of the Aztecs of his interest in gold, but he
did not tell him how valuable the metal was in Europe. The Indians
had so much gold that they did not consider it precious; they only
valued it as a material for their fine craftsmanship. So Cortes ex-
plained to the chief that the Spaniards suffered from a disease that
only gold could cure and that this was why he was so interested in
obtaining the metal.

Among the Aztecs there was a tradition of a white god, Quetzal-
coatl, who had visited them long ago and given them many blessings.
He had then left, promising to return. Now the Aztecs, seeing the
light-skinned Spaniards, came to believe that the gods had returned.
Even Montezuma, the greatest of the Aztec chiefs, believed this.

Pushing further inland, Cortes found several large towns belong-

Sacrificial knife from Mexico is believed to be part of Aztec treasure sent to Spain by Cortes

ing to the Totonacs, who were enemies of Montezuma and the Aztecs. Cortes now realized that the Aztecs dominated many of the neighboring tribes, and that these tribes resented it. He began to play one tribe against the other so that they would not unite against him. For if they did, he knew that all his horses and cannon would not be sufficient to save him.

The Spaniards were amazed and delighted at the richness of the Indian civilization. But they professed to be horrified at some of the more barbaric Indian customs, particularly the practice of human sacrifice. Their horror was no doubt sincere, but it must be remembered that torture and burning alive were still practiced in Spain in the name of Christianity. Nevertheless, the Spanish could not tolerate the paganism of the natives and whenever possible they threw down the Aztec idols and replaced them with the stone cross of their own religion.

Cortes, having gone further into New Spain than any Spaniard before him, began to feel himself more and more independent of Diego Velasquez, who had sent him on the expedition. Some of his men had become unhappy with his leadership and now plotted to steal one of the ships and return to Cuba with a report for Velasquez. But Cortes heard of the plot and sent back word to the coast that all but one of the ships were to be dismantled of sails, lines, and anchors and then sunk. His men were appalled at the thought of being cut off from Cuba, but Cortes managed to persuade them that the vessels were already rotten and worm-eaten. Now they could not turn back.

Their only recourse was to go along with Cortes in his quest for riches toward Montezuma's capital of Tenochtitlan (now Mexico City). The cry went up, "To Mexico! To Mexico!" They could not go home, but riches and honor lay ahead. On August 16, 1519, with an army of 400 men, 15 horses, and 7 artillery pieces hauled by the Indians, they began their long march inland.

In addition to his own men, Cortes had persuaded some 1,300 of the Totonacs to accompany him in his war against Montezuma. He also had about 1,000 slaves to carry his equipment. The rough, winding route led from the dry plains to the heights of the Cordillera Mountains, 7,000 feet above sea level. At the end of August the Spaniards found their way blocked by an army of several thousand Tlaxclan Indians. Though the Tlaxclans were not friendly with the Aztecs, they opposed the Spaniards and refused to let them pass. The Spaniards had to fight their way through. At first the Spaniards were pressed in by high land on either side and could not use their horsemen. But they soon fought their way to level ground where their horses and cannon, both terrifying to the Indians, could be used. At this point, most of the Indians fled.

The day after the battle, the chiefs of the Tlaxclans tried to dissuade Cortes from going further. Failing in this, they offered him 10,000 of their own men to oppose Montezuma. Cortes, fearing that he could not control such a large Indian force, accepted 1,000.

The following week, Cortes reached the city of Cholulu, where he was received without noticeable opposition. But, suspecting treachery among the inhabitants, he slaughtered more than 6,000 of them. The naked Indians, armed with only spears and clubs, were defenceless against the well-armed Spanish. By this slaughter Cortes hoped to terrorize the other Indians so that they would not oppose

Two-headed serpent, another part of the treasure, is made of turquoise

Cortes and his men subdued the capital city and the country of the Aztecs

him. He was successful. News of his victories preceded him all the way to the court of Montezuma, and when he reached the glorious city of Tenochtitlan, he was warmly received by the Emperor of the Aztecs. Montezuma sent gifts of flowers to the Spaniards, and, carried in a litter, went out to meet their leader. He gave them a place in which to quarter their horses and sent them fresh food.

In the following months, Cortes and Montezuma came to like and even admire each other. The Aztec chief had himself once been a great warrior and had often led his people into battle. Now he had become their religious leader as well and exercised almost absolute authority over them. In spite of his friendship for the chief, Cortes felt that it was necessary to assert his own authority. Discovering that some of Montezuma's chiefs were plotting against the Emperor and his Spanish guests, Cortes had five of them burned alive as an example to others. He then seized Montezuma himself and held him prisoner.

It seemed that the Spanish had at last subdued the capital, and with it the country. Cortes ordered that all the Aztec gold be brought to him as tribute. The beautiful gold ornaments of the Aztecs arrived by the basketful and were quickly melted down into slabs for easier carrying. The slabs were divided up among the Spanish officers, and a fifth was sent to the court of Spain. After this, there was little left to distribute among the Spanish soldiers.

Meanwhile, Velasquez in Cuba had heard of Cortes' success in Mexico. He sent a petition to King Charles of Spain, asking permission to go to Mexico and order Cortes back to Cuba. Cortes' great success had aroused the greed and jealousy of Velasquez. The Spanish king was indifferent and ordered one of his courtiers to rule on the petition. This courtier happened to be a friend of Velasquez, and he quickly granted the petition. The Cuban governor gathered a force of 900 men and prepared to leave for Mexico. But word reached him from the government of Santo Domingo, on the island of Hispaniola, forbidding the expedition. Though he was officially subordinate to Santo Domingo, Velasquez ignored the order and dispatched the fleet under the command of Panfilo de Narvaez, a capable veteran of an earlier war.

Despite bad storms in which two ships and 50 men were lost, the fleet reached Cortes' earlier landing place near Vera Cruz. Narvaez sent word to Montezuma that they were on their way to rescue him from Cortes. Montezuma passed on this news to his captors, suggesting that the Spanish, now that they had new ships, could go home. Cortes pretended to agree and set out to meet Narvaez. He sent a messenger ahead explaining that the situation was already dangerous and asking him not to stir up trouble.

Narvaez knew nothing of the conflicts between Cortes and the Aztecs, but he knew that his own Spanish force was larger than that of Cortes. Cortes, realizing that he would have to use every possible trick to overcome this larger force, offered a prize for the man who would capture Narvaez. Cortes reached the camp of Narvaez at night and chose to attack while it was still dark. Narvaez had set out only two sentries; one was caught sleeping, but the other heard Cortes and his men approaching and sounded the alarm. But it was too late to rouse the sleeping men. The battle was a short one. Narvaez was injured in the eye by a lance, and shortly thereafter his inexperienced troops surrendered to Cortes and his veterans. Cortes ordered that all the captured soldiers be set free, except Narvaez and some of his officers. Then, with bribes of gold and promises of glory ahead, Cortes persuaded most of Narvaez' men to join him. They had no choice but to accept.

But almost as soon as he had defeated Narvaez, Cortes received word from Tenochtitlan that the Aztecs had risen against the Spaniards, set fire to the Spanish quarter of the city, and killed several of the soldiers. Cortes turned his army, now augmented by the troops of Narvaez, back toward the mountain city. When he reached the Aztec capital, Montezuma came out to meet him as before, but there was no longer any pretense of friendship between the two men. Cortes immediately made Montezuma a prisoner.

There followed a savage battle in the streets of the city in which many of the Spaniards were slain. It was clear by now that the Aztecs intended to drive the invaders completely from their land. After two days, fighting against an overwhelmingly larger force, the Spaniards reached the foot of the sacred pyramid. In fierce hand-to-hand combat they drove their way up the steps to the peak of the pyramid, where the Aztecs kept the sacred images of their gods. The Spaniards hurled the gods down to the screaming hordes below, then set fire to the structure. The Indians, seeing their gods desecrated and their temple on fire, were terrified.

For weeks the struggle continued. Many more of Narvaez' men came to join Cortes. Indians of other tribes fought alongside the Spanish, hoping to destroy the Aztecs first and drive the Spanish out later. But it seemed impossible to destroy the Aztecs; for every man killed ten others appeared to take his place. Cortes began to realize that his small force would soon be wiped out. In one horrible battle, called *la noche triste* (the woeful night), on June 30, 1520, 450 of the Spanish troops were slain.

Cortes withdrew after this battle and established his camp outside the city. He first planned to retake the capital by attacking it on land and water. But it became clear that cutting a way through the enemy along the narrow causeways leading into the city would be too costly, since the Spanish were too easily outflanked by Aztec

The blood-stained streets of Tenochtitlan saw fierce and bloody battles

warriors in canoes. Cortes needed boats, and fortunately, one of his men was a ship's carpenter. Wood was collected and small flat-bottomed craft were built to suit the shallow water of the cause-ways. Cortes sent to the coast for rigging and sails from the ships he had earlier dismantled.

Meanwhile the Spaniards conquered the surrounding cities to gain supplies and support for the siege of the capital. At some time during the Spanish evacuation of the city, or shortly thereafter, great Montezuma had been killed. Possibly the Spanish killed him as a gesture of revenge. He was succeeded by his nephew and son-in-law Cuauhtemoc, who proceeded to organize resistance.

In April of 1521, the Spanish began their siege of Tenochtitlan. They cut off all food supplies to the city, jammed the canals with waste, and blocked the causeways. The siege went on for 55 days, at the end of which the Indians were too weakened by starvation to resist. The Spaniards entered the city, destroying the idols and shrines of the Aztecs. But the Aztecs, though their organized resistance had been broken, continued to attack the Spaniards in the narrow streets. Cortes decided that the city must be destroyed, house by house. The starving Indians looked on as their beautiful capital was demolished. Not even their young Emperor Cuauhtemoc could put heart into them.

Cortes tried to arrange a meeting with the Aztec leaders, but they failed to appear. The Spaniards then proceeded to slaughter or take prisoner more than 40,000 of the Aztecs. One day, shortly after the burning of the city, the Spanish captured a young Aztec attempting to escape in a canoe. They brought him to Cortes, who recognized him as the Emperor Cuauhtemoc. The young chief was willing to surrender, and the Spanish captain, having taken the city, treated him with courteous consideration. The territory of New Spain belonged to the Spanish at last, after nearly two and a half years of exploration and fighting. On the ruins of Tenochtitlan the Spanish built the new capital of Mexico City.

The Spaniards killed or enslaved thousands of Aztecs in a search for booty to fill their empty treasure chests

The Spaniards wanted to collect their booty and return to Cuba, where many of them had left land and families. Nearly all of them had been wounded at one time or another and, now that the great adventure was over, they wished to go home, nurse their wounds, and live on their newly acquired wealth. They were *conquistadores*, conquerors, and were not skilled at government, which they were quite willing to leave to the Aztecs. Gold was all they wanted. But where had it gone? None, or almost none, was to be found. It had vanished, and to this day no one really knows where. Some claim that the Aztecs had stolen it back and hidden it before the siege; others say that Cortes and his captains hid it from the troops. The Indians said that it had been thrown into the lake. But, wherever it was, it was not recovered.

Aztec stone mask represents a tortured god, Xipe Totec

Cortes now awaited word from Spain as to whether he should remain in Mexico, return to Spain to bring back colonists, or rule the country himself. He sent messages to King Charles and to Velasquez with word of the new colony. But there was much wrangling in the Spanish court as to the legality of Cortes' claim to rule Mexico, and the greedy and jealous Velasquez stirred up as much trouble as he could. Finally word arrived that, as of October, 1522, Cortes should be considered governor, captain-general, and chief justice of the colony, which would be called New Spain. He now had authority to act in the name of King Charles.

Cortes was a skillful governor, ruling the lands he had conquered with so few men for the next 12 years. During this time, he went on expeditions to conquer several territories to the south of New Spain, installing Spanish governments and founding towns. At the end of the 12 years another governor, Antonio de Mendoza, was appointed. Cortes retained his titles, but passed on his authority to his successor.

At the age of 62, Cortes returned to Spain for a final visit. By this time his great strength was exhausted; he died peacefully in his bed in the Spanish city of Seville. His body was taken to Mexico for burial, for he had come to love that conquered country more than his native Spain.

Cortes was perhaps the greatest of the many Spanish *conquista-*

dores who explored and subdued much of South, Central, and North America. He had arrived in New Spain with a force of a little over 600 soldiers. Many of them were not used to taking orders, and most of them were untrained as fighting men. In a series of battles with thousands of Indians, he had lost less than half his force. Cortes led his men personally, enduring with them the hardships of long marches through the jungle and fierce battles in the blood-stained streets of Tenochtitlan.

It may be impossible for us, nowadays, to approve of men like Cortes and the *conquistadores*, but we may at least admire their courage, resourcefulness, and strength.

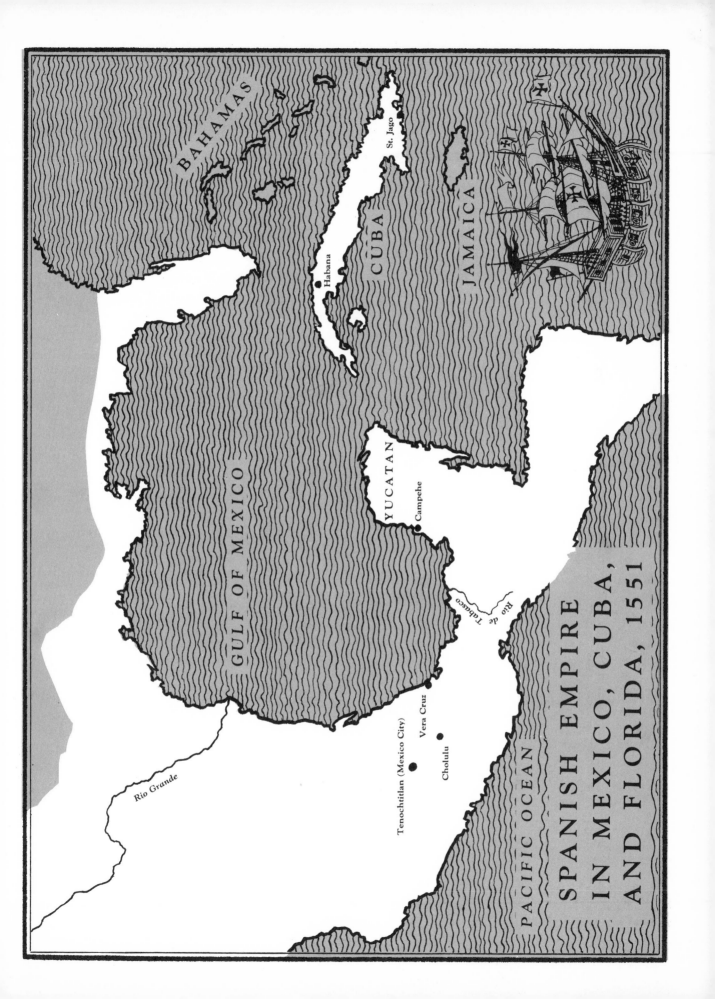

BAHAMAS

St. Jago

CUBA

Habana

JAMAICA

GULF OF MEXICO

YUCATAN

Campehe

Rio de Tabasco

Vera Cruz

Tenochtitlan (Mexico City)

Cholulu

Rio Grande

PACIFIC OCEAN

SPANISH EMPIRE
IN MEXICO, CUBA,
AND FLORIDA, 1551

SWEDEN

WHITE SEA

GULF OF BOTHNIA

FINLAND

BALTIC SEA

St. Petersburg

RUSSIA

PRUSSIA

POLAND

GALICIA

LAKE ARAL

SEA OF AZOV

CRIMEA

BULGARIA

BLACK SEA

CAUCASUS

CASPIAN SEA

OTTOMAN EMPIRE

RUSSIA, 1762

Catherine the Great

The Princess Sophie Augusta Frederica, who was to become Catherine the Great of Russia, was born in the small German principality of Anhalt-Zerbst, the daughter of Prince Christian Augustus. Her mother had wanted a son, and therefore neglected her daughter. The lonely little girl grew up entirely in the care of a French governess.

In 1744, when Sophie was fourteen, her portrait was sent to the powerful Empress Elizabeth of Russia in the hope that Elizabeth would take the young princess into the Russian court and find her a husband. The Empress, who had deposed the rightful heir and usurped the throne, had named as her successor her nephew Peter, Duke of Holstein-Gottorp. Elizabeth, impressed by Sophie's portrait, summoned the girl and her mother to St. Petersburg, and announced the betrothal of Sophie to her nephew, the heir to the throne. A year later, Sophie was baptized into the Russian Orthodox Church and given a new baptismal name—Catherine. She was married to Duke Peter in September, 1745, amidst great pomp and splendor. The public ceremonies celebrating the wedding lasted for 10 days. This marriage was of great political importance, for if Peter, the last male of the Romanov line, should produce a son, the Empress would be more secure on her throne.

Catherine, the once-neglected princess, began to blossom. Witty, vivacious, with sparkling black eyes and a brilliant white complexion, she was the darling of the court; after a year in St. Petersburg, she spoke fluent Russian. But her outstanding intelligence served only to isolate her from the idle and frivolous court. It also estranged her from her childish and stupid young husband. At the age of sixteen, Peter still played with dolls and doted on his toy soldiers. He was so fascinated by the heroic exploits of his neighbor, King Frederick of

Catherine the Great, Empress of Russia

Prussia, that he dressed his valets in Prussian uniforms and drilled them with Prussian words of command. Marriage—if it could be called marriage—had not matured him.

Starved for friendship and bored by her luxurious prison, Catherine took a lover, whose name was Saltykov. Her son Paul, born ten years after her marriage to Peter, may have been the result of this liaison, though the Grand Duke reluctantly acknowledged the child as his own. The Empress Elizabeth snatched the baby almost from the cradle and brought him up as her own. Catherine seldom entered the nursery to see her young son.

Catherine, thrown on her own resources again, set about building a new life. With great patience she embarked on a course of self-education, learning Latin and Greek and corresponding with some of the greatest philosophers of Europe. Through her correspondence with the brilliant Frenchman Voltaire, she became interested in the new trend toward democratic ideas, which was completely at variance with the despotic rule of Russia. While her attempts to apply these ideas to Russia failed, she became known for her attempts at democratic reforms. This was in contrast to her husband, the future Emperor, who still played with his toy soldiers and tried to imitate Frederick of Prussia.

In 1762 the Empress Elizabeth died, and Catherine's husband assumed the throne of Russia as Peter III. At this time, Russia was at war with Prussia, and Peter's admiration for Frederick and all things Prussian made him unpopular. Finally, he withdrew his army from its attack on Prussia, thus betraying his own government. Though he loved to play soldier, he was not up to a real war. And he was even less interested in governing his own country. He began to flaunt his mistresses in public and to talk of divorcing Catherine.

Taking one of his mistresses with him, Peter left St. Petersburg, the capital, and went to his palace at Oranienbaum, where he kept only a small guard. Six months later he was killed in a drunken scuffle. Back in the capital the Regiment of the Guard, which formed the core of the Russian army, recognized Catherine as sole ruler of Russia; this view was shared by most Russian people.

The neglected little princess of a small German principality had become absolute ruler of the largest nation in the civilized world, with power of life and death over its millions of people.

To be Empress of Russia was the goal toward which Catherine had been carefully working for some 18 years. She proceeded quickly to make her position secure. She issued a statement declaring that she had accepted the throne for the good of Russia and, very cautiously at first, began to exercise her new power.

As much as she sympathized with the ideas and ideals of the democratic intellectuals of France, she knew that she owed her real power not to the people of Russia, but to the nobility. And she was an extremely practical woman. Following the forms of democracy, she convened a representative legislature, but allowed it no authority. She thought of alleviating the wretched condition of the peasants but when an uprising occurred under a peasant named Pugachev, she put it down with ruthless slaughter. And when, toward the end of her life, the French Revolution broke out, she actively opposed it.

But, though her commitment to the democratic ideals then growing in the West was only superficial, she did encourage the importation of Western culture into Russia. She brought masterpieces of painting and sculpture from all over Europe and invited Western scholars to live at her court.

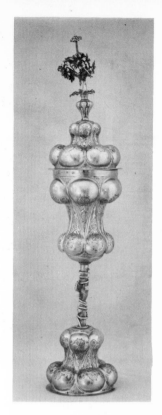

Above: Silver goblet used in Russia during Catherine's era.
Lower: Gilded standing cup comes from 18th-century Russia

Painting of Catherine, the young wife of Duke Peter. It was completed in 1748 by Georg Christoph Grooth

The court, which had once been slovenly and barbaric, became the most brilliant and enlightened in Europe. Catherine encouraged her important nobles to travel and broaden their education. She surrounded herself with artists, writers, and musicians, and spent some time learning to paint and to write witty little comedies which were performed at court. But perhaps her main contribution to the amusement of her court was her private life, which was the cause of constant gossip.

Catherine had to rule a people of varied races, cultures, and traditions. There was no surer way of holding their admiration and loyalty than by making war. The wars going on in Europe at the time gave her numerous opportunities to do this. In 1772 she took part in the first partition of Poland, engineered by Frederick of Prussia. By this she added considerable territory—White Russia and all the land westward to the Dnieper and Dvina rivers—and gained access to the Black Sea. In 1793, she took part in a second partition of Poland which allowed free entry of Russian troops into Poland and established Russian control over Polish foreign policy.

The Empress was a prodigious worker, rising at five in the morning, often making her own fire, so that she could deal with her voluminous correspondence before the official day began. She played as vigorously as she worked; she loved gaiety and witty conversation, and was particularly fond of any man who could amuse her. The widowed Empress took many lovers, discarding them when they ceased to amuse. One of these was the near-genius Potemkin, whose wit, mimicry, and intelligence fascinated her.

In 1783, an intermittent war with the Ottoman Empire resulted in Russia's seizure of the Crimea. Catherine named Potemkin prince of the territory and installed him as governor.

Forced to live far from Catherine and her glittering capital, Potemkin amused himself by writing her glowing accounts of his reforms and achievements. He told of new vineyards already bearing fruit, herds of cattle grazing on grassy meadows, strong new fortresses garrisoned by whole armies trained and ready for battle.

Leaders of the Ottoman Empire receive Prince Repnin, special ambassador from Catherine, who won Turkish lands providing outlets to the sea

*Silhouette on glass, executed in Russia
during late 1700's, represents the Empress
who brought the best of Western
culture to her country*

The trouble was that none of this was true. The Crimea was still as poor and barren as it had been when Potemkin arrived. But Catherine, fired by his enthusiastic letters, decided that she must see these wonders with her own eyes. Potemkin, naturally enough, was most unhappy to hear that she planned to visit him. If she discovered that his reports had been completely false, he would lose his high position, and might also lose his life.

Potemkin proceeded to deceive the Empress with one of the most amazing hoaxes in history. He turned the route the Empress was to take into a scene which fulfilled the expectations his letters had aroused. Accompanied by some 3,000 of her court and guards, the Empress drove day after day over hastily made roads that would vanish with the first rain, between avenues of flowering trees that would die in the desert soil soon after she had admired them; within sight of fat herds of cattle that were driven on to be viewed again farther down the road. Moveable houses, or rather house fronts like movie sets, were assembled into villages, disassembled and made into other villages further on. Frowning fortresses of mud and sand gave an impression of solid military power, but crumbled away shortly after the Empress passed by.

Catherine was completely deceived. Feasted, flattered, entertained, and amused, she did not bother to examine Potemkin's stagecraft at close quarters. She returned happily to St. Petersburg, and Potemkin's cardboard empire reverted to desolate reality.

At the age of 61, Empress Catherine, now a fat old woman, received news of the French Revolution. Once she had been on good terms with the thinkers whose ideas had helped bring the revolution about. But the violent overthrow of the monarchy, the wholesale murders and bloody excesses which accompanied the uprising had little in common with her polite, theoretical liberalism. Like the other rulers of Europe, liberal or otherwise, she was appalled at the thought that what had happened to the King of France might happen to her.

Louis XVI was executed on January 21, 1793 and soon after, Prussia and Austria declared war on France. In 1793 Britain, Holland, and Spain joined in, but it was not until 1796 that Catherine mustered an army of 150,000 to march against France. She did not live to see the end of this campaign. She died at the age of 67, on the day that the news of Napoleon's victory over the Austrians at Arcola reached St. Petersburg.

Catherine the Great ruled court and country with strong determination

As Empress, Catherine had done little to reform her fast-rambling empire, despite her democratic ideas. But she did bring enlightenment to its center, the court at St. Petersburg.

The little German princess, who, almost single-handed, won for herself the largest empire of her day, had worked with courage, intelligence, and undeviating purpose to become one of the makers of history. Like Elizabeth I of England, she coupled an almost masculine determination with the feminine qualities of patience, secrecy, and even flirtation. She led a varied, vigorous, and sometimes chaotic personal life, but she never let it get in the way of her first love, which was for the country she ruled.

SWEDEN

WHITE SEA

GULF OF BOTHNIA

FINLAND

BALTIC SEA

St. Petersburg

RUSSIA

PRUSSIA

POLAND

GALICIA

LAKE ARAL

SEA OF AZOV

CRIMEA

CASPIAN SEA

BULGARIA

BLACK SEA

CAUCASUS

OTTOMAN EMPIRE

RUSSIA, 1801

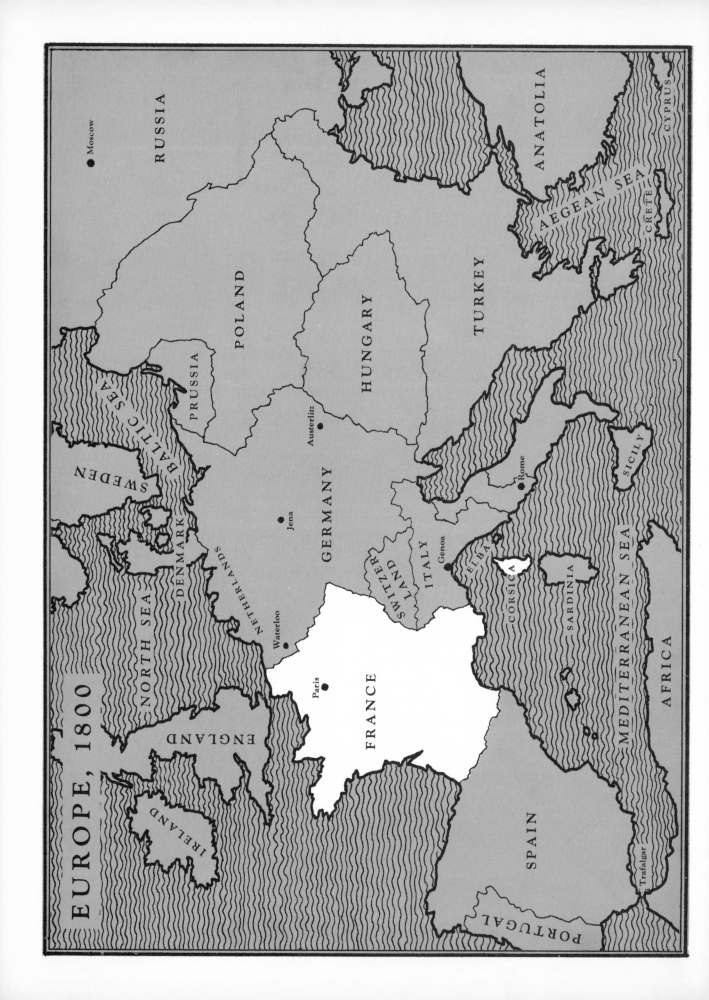

EUROPE, 1800

RUSSIA
Moscow

POLAND

PRUSSIA

BALTIC SEA

SWEDEN

DENMARK

NETHERLANDS

NORTH SEA

ENGLAND

IRELAND

Waterloo

Jena

GERMANY

HUNGARY

Austerlitz

SWITZER LAND

ITALY

Genoa

ELBA

CORSICA

SARDINIA

Rome

SICILY

MEDITERRANEAN SEA

AFRICA

TURKEY

ANATOLIA

AEGEAN SEA

CRETE

CYPRUS

Paris

FRANCE

SPAIN

PORTUGAL

Trafalgar

Napoleon Bonaparte

Few characters in history have been so controversial as the thin, dark, little Corsican who rose to be sovereign of one of the world's greatest empires. Over a hundred thousand books have been written about his character, his rise to power, his victorious campaigns, and his final defeat and imprisonment. To some he is one of the great heroes of the world; to others, he is a monster. But those who admire him and those who hate him are equally fascinated by his career.

Napoleon was born on August 15, 1769, in Ajaccio, Corsica. He was the third son of Letizia Ramolina and Carlo Maria Buonaparte (Napoleon later changed the family name to Bonaparte). Corsica, an island lying in the Mediterranean, had been ruled by the Italian city of Genoa until shortly before Napoleon's birth. His father Carlo had fought for Corsican independence from Genoa. But when Genoa could not put down the rebellion, France stepped in and subjugated the island. Carlo Buonaparte, realizing that independence was now a lost cause, became an active collaborationist with the French. His support of French rule won him the favor of the French King Louis XVI, and it was through the King's patronage that Napoleon, then ten years old, was sent to a military school at Brienne. Later, he and his brother Joseph enrolled in the Military College near Paris. There, Napoleon received a solid education as an artillery officer, with special studies in modern warfare.

When Napoleon's father died in 1785, Joseph, as the eldest son, should have become head of the family. But Napoleon found his brother too frivolous to assume this responsibility and himself undertook to provide for his mother, four younger brothers and two sisters.

In 1789, the French Revolution broke out and with it the Reign

Napoleon Bonaparte, Emperor of France

of Terror. King Louis XVI was deposed and he and his queen, Marie Antoinette, were executed. Some of the nobility were either executed or driven into exile. In 1792, Napoleon, already an officer in the French army, returned to Corsica on family business. He over-stayed his leave and narrowly escaped being shot as a deserter. Luck was with him on this occasion, as it was to be on greater occasions throughout his career. The revolutionary government appointed Napoleon Captain of the Guard in Corsica. But shortly thereafter, the Buonapartes fled Corsica and went to the city of Toulon on the mainland. At Toulon, Napoleon was raised to the rank of brigadier general, another rare stroke of luck.

In 1795, the fifth government since 1789 broke up and was replaced by a new regime called the Directory. The Directory put down several insurrections within France and in general restored a measure of stability to the country's political life. But opposition to the revolutionary government was active outside of France. To protect their territories from French invasion, and to insure that France would not serve as a breeding ground for revolution in their own countries, several nations had, in 1792, formed the First Coalition. The Coalition consisted of Prussia, Austria, Spain, England, Portugal, and several smaller powers, along with numerous members of the French upper classes who had been driven out of the country.

At this time, Napoleon's luck had taken a turn for the worse. He was in Paris, jobless, with little money and seeking his fortune.

Then he met the woman who was to share with him the triumphs of his rise to power—the glamorous Josephine de Beauharnais, a woman of mixed French and Negro blood from the French island of Martinique, off South America. Josephine's husband had been guillotined during the Reign of Terror, leaving his widow almost penniless, with two small children. Napoleon fell in love with her and within a few months of their first meeting married her.

Shortly after his marriage, Napoleon was given command of the French army in Italy, which was fighting the Austrian army for control of the northern part of the country. The Directory had thought of the Italian campaign as only a small part of the war with the First Coalition. It was Napoleon's drive for glory that turned it into a major victory.

On taking command of his forces north of the Alps, he addressed the 38,000 troops: "You are badly fed and all but naked," he told them. "I am about to lead you into the most fertile plains in the world, where we will find honor, glory and riches."

Some weeks later, Napoleon's army engaged the Austrians at Millesimo and defeated them. He went on to win the battles of Mondovè and Lodi and, on May 15, 1796, he entered Milan in triumph. From Milan he went on to conquer all of Lombardy as far as Mantua. Without costing the French treasury a sou—the French army had lived off the wealth of the land they conquered—Napoleon had turned a minor campaign into a great victory. He sent a treasure in gold, silver, and art objects back to Paris and himself made a fortune of about $3,000,000 out of the victory.

Napoleon went on to win other victories against the Coalition in Italy and Germany. Finally, in the Treaty of Campo Formio on October 11, 1797, Austria ceded Belgium and the left bank of the Rhine to France. England, however, refused to go along with the

Napoleon vowed to lead his troops onward to "honor, glory and riches"

terms of the treaty, and the only way to obtain her consent would be to invade and conquer her. But since an invasion at this point was out of the question, Napoleon decided to attack the British empire in India, by way of Egypt. There was one great weakness in this scheme. France had no navy, whereas England, which had Horatio Nelson in command of the fleet, dominated the seas.

Nevertheless, the French army set sail from Toulon with 400 vessels. They slipped by the British fleet, which had sought refuge from a storm in the nearest harbor, and landed in Egypt in July, 1798. Nelson had lost contact with the French fleet during July, but found them on August 1 in the harbor of Abukir, east of Alexandria. The French were cornered and outnumbered, and Nelson was able to destroy their fleet without much trouble. Napoleon and his army were thus cut off from France, without supplies or means of retreat.

Napoleon then engaged the British army of Egypt near Alexandria and defeated them. But the young general did not know how to turn a single victory into conquest. Before long plague broke out among the French, and Napoleon, claiming that he was needed back in France, slipped aboard a ship and returned to Europe.

While Napoleon was in Egypt, a new alliance, called the Second Coalition, had been formed against France. The most important members were Russia, England, Austria, Naples, Portugal, and the Ottoman (Turkish) Empire. They planned a triple offensive to force the French out of Italy in the south, the Netherlands in the north, and Germany in the east. In October, 1799, the British were defeated at Alkmaar in the Netherlands. They withdrew to England, leaving the Austrian, Russian, and allied armies alone to fight Napoleon on the continent. By now, the victories of the French army under Napoleon had made him the terror of Europe, and particularly of England.

But if the French army was victorious, the Directory govern-ment which it served was in complete confusion. Finances were in a wretched state. The people were weary of war and the resulting lack of food. There was even talk of recalling the monarchy. Napo-leon, who had been asked to travel back to France by influential people, decided to turn toward Paris.

The victorious general was greeted with wild acclaim. He was strong where the Directory was weak; he was a soldier of the revolu-tion, whereas the Bourbon monarchs would only bring back the system against which the people had risen in 1789. In November, 1799, Napoleon overthrew the Directory and replaced it with a new government—the Consulate, with himself as First Consul. As First Consul, he now held almost complete power. There were two other Consuls, but their job was simply to advise Napoleon, not to make policy.

Ornate parade helmet belonged to King Louis XIV, grandfather of the last Bourbon monarch

Young Napoleon in 1798 could not turn victory in Egypt into conquest

In December, 1799, Napoleon submitted a new constitution to the French people. It was approved by an overwhelming majority. Aside from providing for the three consuls, with an all-powerful First Consul, the constitution established three legislative bodies, the Tribunate, the Senate, and the Legislative Chamber. But these bodies could do little more than discuss and approve the First Consul's policies.

Napoleon's new constitution also reorganized the administration and finances of the country by breaking it up into administrative units and establishing a new system of tax collection. The new administrative system proved to be highly efficient—so efficient that most of it has been retained to the present day.

Napoleon, now supreme head of France, began to see himself as a second Julius Caesar. Like Caesar, he had won great foreign battles for his country and then returned to become her leader. He planned to re-establish the "natural frontiers" of France, based on the borders of the ancient Roman province of Gaul, and even to go beyond them to capture the surrounding countries.

Needless to say, the other countries were not at all enthusiastic about Napoleon's scheme. The countries of the Second Coalition renewed the warfare which had begun in 1798. This time, however, they were defending themselves not so much against revolutionary France as against Napoleon himself.

In May, 1800, after a horrible famine in the city, Genoa fell to the French. Napoleon then crossed from France into Italy through the St. Bernard Pass in the Alps to attack the Austrians, who had retreated from the French army at Genoa. The crossing was one of the most difficult feats of Napoleon's early career. Forty thousand men had to march through the pass, hauling their artillery in hollow trunks—the snow was too deep for horses.

On June 14, Napoleon met the Austrian army at Marengo and defeated it. Meanwhile, the rest of the French army had won victories in Germany and Italy, and Austria was unable to continue the war. Austria conceded defeat in the Treaty of Luneville, in which she ceded to France most of her territories in Italy, Switzerland and Germany.

In the next few months, Napoleon signed treaties with England and Naples and with the Pope. This was the end of the Second Coalition, and there now began a brief period of peace.

Napoleon used this breathing spell to make further changes at home. He invited the nobility to return from exile and presided over a glittering society in Paris. He established the Legion of Honor, France's most coveted decoration, proclaimed the Civil Code, still the basis of French law, and established the University of Paris in its present form.

On August 2, 1802, Napoleon was declared Consul for life, with the right to choose his successor. He dropped the Bonaparte from his name, preferring to use only his first name, in the style of the old royalty.

On May 18, 1804, Napoleon took the final step in his rise to power—he was proclaimed Emperor. He might have called himself King, but that term carried echoes of the banished Bourbons. In any case, "Emperor" was more impressive. It was the title of his hero Julius Caesar, and of Charlemagne, the first Holy Roman Emperor.

Elaborate fowling piece was made especially for Napoleon

Napoleon, like his hero Julius Caesar, became Emperor of his domain

Like Charlemagne, Napoleon wished to be crowned by the Pope, and the ceremony took place on December 2, almost six months after the proclamation. To demonstrate his independence, Napoleon took the crown from the Pope's hands and placed it on his own head. He also crowned Josephine Empress.

During the months of peace, Napoleon had kept an army at Boulogne in preparation for an invasion of England, which had still not accepted the treaties whereby Napoleon had won most of western Europe. He had earlier delayed invading beyond the English Channel—probably because it was almost impossible—and now, as Emperor, he turned his attention to other conquests.

He was not satisfied with the "natural frontiers" he had first set out to establish. He now spoke of conquering not only Europe, but Constantinople and even North America. His sole aim was glory, and his craving for glory began to have less and less to do with reality. Indeed, some historians have declared that he was mad. But mad or not, Napoleon's conquests and the hint of even greater glories to come turned Paris into the glittering capital that it had been before the Revolution. The court dazzled with great names; titles (most of them created by the Emperor) and trappings abounded. Josephine, the "creole adventuress," was a gracious empress, but, in her own way, she was as eccentric as her husband, spending wildly, buying jewels, fine furniture, and paintings, turning her home, La Malmaison, into an ornate treasure house. Napoleon gave elaborate state dinners, but his behavior was less than gracious. He would often keep his guests waiting for hours, then rush in and bolt his food in ten minutes, scarcely speaking to a guest, and then rush off again.

In 1804 the Emperor resumed his preparations for an invasion of England. He planned to augment the army that had been waiting at Boulogne and turn it into an immense expeditionary force. To transport the army, he built thousands of flat barges. But meanwhile his old enemies were forming another alliance against him—the Third

Coronation in Paris of Napoleon as Emperor and Josephine as Empress

Coalition consisting of England, Austria, Russia, and Sweden. Napoleon broke up his camp at Boulogne and marched his expeditionary force, which he had named the Grand Army, toward Vienna to meet the Austrian forces.

But on October 21, 1805, France suffered a major loss. The English navy, commanded by Lord Nelson who had defeated the French in Egypt, attacked the French fleet at Trafalgar. Nelson was killed during the battle, but not before defeating the French and making Britain the undisputed mistress of the seas for the next hundred years. Napoleon had now lost the ships with which he had planned to invade England. But shortly after this defeat at sea, he won a major victory on land.

A fresh army of Austrians and Russians was massed at Austerlitz. The Russians were commanded by Czar Alexander I and the Austrians by their ruler Francis I. Thus, three emperors were leading their countries' forces, and the Battle of Austerlitz became known as the Battle of the Three Emperors. Napoleon defeated the Austrians and forced the Russians to retreat. In the treaty that followed, Austria ceded many of her German and Italian possessions to France. Napoleon quickly consolidated his power in Italy by appointing his older brother, Joseph, King of the Two Sicilies. He then appointed another brother, Louis, King of the Netherlands. The maps show how much territory Napoleon had added to France.

France's next great victory was against the Prussians at Jena, where he impressively defeated them. Now, having conquered

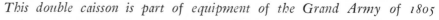

This double caisson is part of equipment of the Grand Army of 1805

Napoleon, in characteristic dress, reviews a formation of infantry soldiers

Prussia and Austria and forced the English army off the Continent, Napoleon felt that he must win Russia as well. But first he took steps to keep the English at bay and to drive the Russian army back within its own borders. To deal with England, he closed all European ports to her ships, preventing her from carrying on any trade with the continent. Napoleon then signed a treaty with Russia by which the Russian army was to withdraw from East Prussia and Poland and he was to control these territories.

The problem of Russia was solved for the moment. The Emperor now turned his attention to Spain and Portugal, where his government was beset by popular rebellions. He had placed his brother on the throne of the two countries, and this turned out to be one of his greatest blunders. The Spanish rose against him, and at Vimeiro, with the help of Sir Arthur Wellesley (later the Duke of Wellington), defeated the French army of occupation. But in the next four years, the French recovered from this defeat and regained their power in Spain and Portugal.

Napoleon was now Emperor of the French and ruler of much

of Europe. His empire also included several islands in the Caribbean and the vast Louisiana Territory in North America. But he still had one problem. Josephine had not given him a son to inherit the Empire. So in 1810, he divorced Josephine and married the Archduchesse Marie Louise, daughter of the Austrian Emperor Francis I. On March 20, 1811, Napoleon's new wife bore him a son. At his birth, the boy was named King of Rome.

Having defeated his enemies in western Europe and established cordial relations with Austria by marrying a member of the ruling family, Napoleon now turned to the conquest of Russia. With an army of 600,000, the greatest one then in Europe, he fought his way across Poland and western Russia, driving the Czar's army before him. He destroyed the city of Smolensk and, in an extremely bloody battle, held the Russians at Borodino. The Russians were forced to retreat to Moscow, and then to abandon it. Napoleon occupied the city on September 14, but that triumph was his last in the Russian campaign. For the Russians set fire to the city, whose buildings were made mostly of wood, and burned it to the ground. Napoleon now had no supplies and no shelter for his troops. And he was so far from France that no supplies could be transported to him.

On October 19, he ordered a retreat from Moscow. His men were forced to march through a barren winter wasteland, where they were harassed constantly by small bands of Russian soldiers and guerrillas. Men died by the thousands, of disease, of wounds, of starvation and cold. Crossing Poland and Germany, the once great army of invasion broke up into bands of foragers and looters. They had numbered 600,000; now fewer than 100,000 remained. Napoleon left his troops and returned to Paris, arriving on December 18. At about the same time, the survivors of his army began to straggle across the Russian border.

Napoleon was able to rally a small army of some 14,000, but now all Europe had turned against him. Prussia, Sweden, Germany, and Holland joined forces against the French, adding their power to that of Austria. The Russians remained neutral for a time, but eventually joined forces against Napoleon. In the Battle of the Nations, fought near Leipzig in October, 1813, the combined armies of these powers defeated the French and forced them back into French territory. About a year later, the victorious armies of the allies entered Paris.

Napoleon, in an attempt to save what he could of the Empire, abdicated in favor of his son Francis Joseph Charles, who was to rule as Napoleon II. But the allies rejected this solution, and Napoleon was forced to give up his throne unconditionally.

This should have been the end of Napoleon's career. But the allies who had defeated him could not agree on what sort of peace they wanted and what new boundaries should be established. The delegates to the peace conference quarreled among themselves for weeks and finally decided to permit the restoration of the old monarchy. Louis XVIII, the brother of Louis XVI, who had been beheaded during the Revolution, assumed the throne. But the French people did not favor restoration of the monarchy, and Louis XVIII was a less than efficient ruler. Before long, the government and the economy were in great confusion.

Napoleon had been packed off to the island of Elba, where he retained the title of Emperor and ruled a little kingdom all his own.

Before his own final defeat, Napoleon salutes troops he has just beaten

In March, 1815, about eleven months after Louis XVIII had become King, Napoleon gambled that the people had had enough of the new monarchy and that the time was ripe for invasion. He easily dodged the ships that guarded his island prison and landed at Cannes on the French mainland with 1,500 men. French troops were sent to oppose him, but they quickly rallied to his cause. On March 20, Napoleon arrived in Paris and the King fled.

Now began the last period of Napoleon's rule, known as the Hundred Days. Austria, England, Prussia, the Netherlands, and Russia concluded a new alliance against Napoleon, each agreeing to supply forces for a large army, under the command of the Duke of Wellington who, years earlier, had defeated the French in Spain. The armies met at Waterloo on June 18, 1815. Napoleon had struck swiftly, hoping for a quick victory which would discourage the allies. He almost succeeded. The British and Dutch under Wellington held out for most of the day under a furious French assault. But toward the end of the day they were beginning to weaken. Marshall Blücher, however, arrived leading the Prussian army to aid the British. Against such a force the French had no chance and they were completely routed.

From this special observation tower at Waterloo, Napoleon watched his troops engage combined European forces commanded by the Duke of Wellington

The battle at Waterloo in 1815 was Napoleon's final bid for power

Napoleon was now ordered to leave the country, this time under heavy guard. On board the British ship *Bellerophon* he was taken to the lonely tropical island of St. Helena, far off the coast of southwest Africa. Here he died seven years later.

Napoleon had conquered most of Europe, had briefly extended his power to Moscow in the east and Egypt in the south, and had purchased large territories in North America. And he had lost it all.

The clue to his brilliant rise to power and to his ultimate defeat seems to be that he was an opportunist and little else. As an opportunist, he took advantage of any situation that served his purpose, regardless of the cost to his own country or to neighboring countries. This quality made him a brilliant tactician, but a poor strategist. Strategy is the art of planning wars and battles far in advance; tactics is the art of moving men and equipment about once the battle has begun. Napoleon won many battles by his brilliant tactics. But he failed in his larger schemes, such as the invasion of Russia, because of his poor strategy.

He was too much of a wishful thinker, too confident of his luck and of himself to possess the cold, objective mind of a great strategist.

The characteristics that made him a poor strategist also made him a poor statesman. On several occasions he could have made peace with his enemies on terms most favorable to France. But that would only have benefited his war-torn country, not his grand ambitions, and Napoleon was more an egotist than a patriot. He believed in his "star," his destiny, and little else. Other leaders have made war out of dedication to a country, a religion, or an ideal. Napoleon, it seems, fought all his battles for himself.

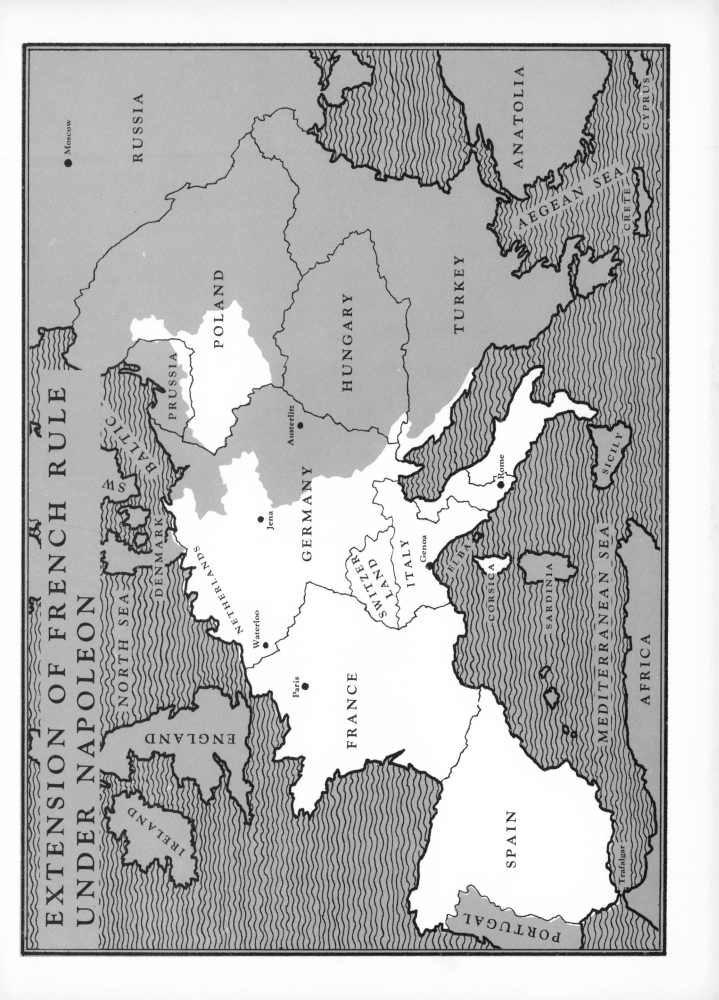

EXTENSION OF FRENCH RULE
UNDER NAPOLEON

RUSSIA

Moscow

POLAND

HUNGARY

ANATOLIA

CYPRUS

AEGEAN SEA

CRETE

TURKEY

PRUSSIA

BALTIC

SW

Austerlitz

DENMARK

NETHERLANDS

GERMANY

Jena

SWITZER LAND

ITALY

Genoa

Rome

ELBA

SICILY

CORSICA

SARDINIA

NORTH SEA

Waterloo

ENGLAND

Paris

FRANCE

MEDITERRANEAN SEA

AFRICA

IRELAND

SPAIN

Trafalgar

PORTUGAL

Suggested Reading

BAKER, GEORGE, *Justinian*. New York: Dodd, Mead, 1931.

BERNSTEIN, PAUL, AND GREEN, ROBERT W., *History of Civilization, vol. 1*. Totowa, New Jersey: Littlefield, Adams, 1965.

DOWNEY, GLANVILLE, *Constantinople in the Age of Justinian*. Norman, Oklahoma: University of Oklahoma Press, 1960.

DURANT, WILL, *The Story of Civilization*. New York: Simon and Schuster, 1965.

FREEMAN, EDWARD AUGUSTUS, *The Ottoman Power in Europe*. London: Macmillan, 1877.

GUERARD, ALBERT L., *Napoleon I, A Great Life in Brief*. New York: Alfred A. Knopf, Inc., 1956.

HASKINS, CHARLES H., *The Normans in European History*. New York: Frederick Ungar, 1959.

HEROLD, J. CHRISTOPHER, *The Age of Napoleon*. New York: Harper & Row, 1963.

KAIS, G., *Portrait of Catherine*. New York: Viking, 1935.

KOMROFF, MANUEL, *Napoleon*. New York: Messner, 1954.

LAMB, HAROLD, *Charlemagne: The Legend and the Man*. New York: Doubleday, 1954.

LANGER, WILLIAM L., *ed., Encyclopedia of World History, rev. ed.* Boston: Houghton Mifflin Company, 1952.

LINKLATER, ERIC, *The Conquest of England*. New York: Doubleday, 1966.

LORD, JOHN, *Charlemagne*. New York: Fords, Howard and Hulbert, 1896.

MATTESON, ROBERT, *comp., The Corsican: A Diary of Napoleon's Life in His Own Words*. Boston: Houghton Mifflin, 1910.

MUIR, WILLIAM, *The Caliphate: Its Rise, Decline and Fall*. Mystic, Connecticut: Verry, Lawrence, 1965.

OLDENBOURG, ZOE, *Catherine the Great*, trans. by A. Carter. New York: Pantheon, 1965.

OROSIUS, PAULUS, *Seven Books of History Against the Pagans*, trans. by R. J. Deferrari. Washington, D.C.: Catholic University of America Press, 1964.

PAINTER, SIDNEY, *French Chivalry*. Baltimore: Johns Hopkins Press, 1940.

PRESCOTT, WILLIAM H., *The Conquest of Mexico*. New York: E. P. Dutton, 1909.

ROBINSON, JAMES HARVEY, *Readings in Modern European History*. Boston: Ginn, 1908-09.

RODWELL, JOHN M., trans., *Koran*. London: J. M. Dent, 1937.

SLOCUMB, GEORGE, *William the Conqueror*. New York: G. P. Putnam, 1961.

STONG, PHILIP D., *Marta of Muscovy, the Fabulous Life of Russia's First Empress*. New York: Doubleday, Doran, 1945.

THATCHER, OLIVER J., and MCNEAL, E. H., *A Source Book for Medieval History*. New York: Scribner, 1905.

VAN SICKLE, CLIFTON E., *A Political and Cultural History of the Ancient World, vol. 1*. Boston: Houghton Mifflin, 1948.

WELLS, H. G., *Outline of History, rev. ed*. New York: Doubleday, 1956.

Index

Huron School Library
Huron, Ohio

920   4779
B   Berry, Erick
      Men who changed the map

McComb Library
McCormick School

920   93   4779
B   Berry, Erick,

McComb Library
McCormick School
      Men Who Changed the Map

Date Due

JA 25 '73			
FE 7 73			
22 '73			
DEC 1 9 19			

Huron School Library
Huron, Ohio